Fragments
of My Fleece

Books by Dean Acheson

DEAN ACHESON

Fragments
of My Fleece

‹‹‹‹‹

W · W · NORTON & COMPANY · INC

NEW YORK

To B. E.

"to whom I owe thanks for gathering these little
fragments of my fleece that I have left upon the
hedges of life."

Contents

9

Contents

Part One ⫷

Idle Thoughts

This Simian World

A little less than half a century ago, when this small book by Clarence Day was published, Mr. Justice Holmes said to me that in its few pages would be found as much insight into human nature and shrewd wisdom as in a good many volumes of philosophy and anthropology. How often I have thought of his remark since! As I have sat through many hours of meetings of foreign ministers and of the General Assembly of the United Nations, I have consoled myself with an observation of Clarence Day's: "Whatever a simian does," he has written here, "there must always be some talking about it. He can't even make peace without a kind of chatter called a peace conference. Super-cats would not have had to 'make' peace: they would have just walked off and stopped

Introduction to *This Simian World* by Clarence Day (New York: Alfred A. Knopf, 1968).

fighting." As Vishinsky would wander on hour after hour, one could turn off the translation and contemplate that dialectical materialism was purely simian, a use of the ape-man's great discovery, talk, to addle his poor brains.

Another of Mr. Day's gems of wisdom still brings me comfort when, sitting in council, despair creeps over me and the tools of analysis seem to be more association of ideas and instinctive response than reason. As the first twinges of reasoned thought began to compete with instinct as a guide to conduct, Day pictures his "poor far-off brother" "perched in his tree, torn between these two voices, wailing loudly at night by a river, in his puzzled distress." One can hear closer brothers, still torn between these two voices, wailing beside another river called the Potomac.

This Simian World is satire of the purest Swiftian style, but gentler. Whereas Gulliver traveled far and met many sizes, shapes, and manner of men to throw light on the human comedy, Clarence Day travels back in time to examine the species existing "after the great saurians had been swept from the scene" and to pick a winner in the evolutionary sweepstakes. Some are ruled out at once: horses, as too timid; seals, as too trustful; cows, as too exploitable. Dogs had more spirit, but more love than integrity—true to others but not to themselves. The most obvious contestants were the ants or bees, the cats, and the elephants; but each would have suffered in the race from the defects of its qualities: the ants, from excessive order and selflessness; the cats, from excessive craftiness, which would study "the world calculatingly, from without, instead of understandingly from within . . . not simply to know but to circumvent the universe"; the elephants, from excessive contemplation and too great magnanimity. In each case he draws pictures (both literally and figuratively) of these civilizations, pictures that are sheer delight but in many respects frightening and perplexing (from a simian point of view).

Recently on a visit to the space center at Cape Kennedy, I wished that Clarence Day could have been along to see how impossible the Apollo shot would have been for super-cat-men. Their curiosity would not have carried them that far. To them the amazing effort and ingenuity put into that effort would have been aimless indeed. The judgment of the Cats-in-Council would have been, "There's no catnip in it." It is the simian's insatiable curiosity, his irresistible desire to monkey around, that produces pure research. Aimless, disinterested research is to us the highest and most essential pursuit of scientific knowledge. Journeymen can apply its discoveries to machine tools, space travel, and nylon stockings.

Curiosity versus disorder was the basic problem of the ape-men, as it is ours. "Their minds will be full enough. Their intelligence will be active and keen. It will have a constant tendency, however, to outstrip their wisdom." We see this tendency around us in our dealings with our environment, ourselves, and our relations with other groups. Then, too, "the simians are always being stirred by desire and passion . . .

Idle Thoughts

Other species have times and seasons for sexual matters, but the simian-folk are thus preoccupied all the year round." Clarence Day examines the phenomenon that fascinates the hippies with a lighter touch than they do. "Will it kill us or save us? Will this trait and our insatiable curiosity interact on each other?" A good question, Senator. Unfortunately, further deponent sayeth not.

"Are we or are we not simians? . . . If we are fallen angels, we should go this road: if we are super-apes, that." The discussion of this problem is what Justice Holmes found worth the volumes of philosophy. Like philosophy it gives no answers, but points roads, and leaves us with a tantalizing last sentence: "If we wanted to *be* Gods—but ah, can we grasp that ambition?"

Random Harvest

Life for all of us has been so concentrated on the immediate in these past years—each day with its pressing task; each meeting with its agenda; each conversation with its urgent need for relevancy—that one faces a gathering which is not going to end in a vote with a sense of emptiness. For it takes a wise man and the long habit of contemplation to spin threads from one's own innards. The rest of us can only splice those odd fragments of conclusion which this unaccustomed effort produces.

The first task is repression. One who has been serving in the field of foreign affairs must beware at a moment like this of those "pernicious abstractions," in the Lincolnian phrase, which rise in the heart and gather to the eyes—albeit only the mind's eyes. Sov-

Address delivered at a dinner of the Associated Harvard Clubs, Copley Plaza Hotel, Boston, Mass., June 4, 1946.

17

Idle Thoughts

ereignty, security—in a curious way so many of them begin with s—selfishness, survival, sacrifice, self-executing, society, social significance, and suicide. The "inters" also dig a pit for the unwary—interdependent, international, inextricably intermingled. We turn to them from an almost biological urge to stretch from where we are to somewhere brighter, like a sprout coming through the earth. But speeches in which they appear usually portray a mood rather than a thought, and are apt to end with a paraphrase of the closing sentence of the Gettysburg Address.

If one is to spin from his own visceral wisdom, he must say, first, "I shall not be a fake"; and, second, "What do I know, or think I know, from my own experience and not by literary osmosis?" An honest answer would be, "Not much; and I am not too sure of most of it."

One thing, however, seems pretty sure—that the tasks which grow out of the relations of our country with other countries are hard ones. This does not come from any lack of ideas and suggestions. These pour out on the unhappy laborer in this vineyard in a generous, if varied, flood. Mr. Morrow remarked that there were two classes of people: those who talked about things, and those who did things. And he added that the competition in the second group was not keen.

No, the difficulty does not come from any meagerness of choice of direction or method. It comes pretty directly from the medium with which one works, the human animal himself. Senator Barkley observes resignedly from time to time that one man has about as much human nature as another—and perhaps a little more. And so, when we tackle the fundamental task in the conduct of our foreign affairs, which Mr. Hull has described as focusing the will of a hundred and forty million people on problems beyond our shores, we find ourselves in trouble. The trouble comes from the fact that people are focusing on a hundred and forty million other things—or, more accurately, not focusing on them, but getting very much mixed up with and about them—and the people in other countries are doing the same thing.

The reasons why this is so lie beyond the limits of my knowledge and so talk about them is banned by my self-restraining ordinance. But there is one contributing factor which I have observed and believe causes an immense amount of trouble. Man has been poking about with his own mind and has found out too much about it for his own wisdom to handle.

For a long time we have gone along with some well-tested principles of conduct: That it was better to tell the truth than falsehoods; that a half truth was no truth at all; that duties were older than and as fundamental as rights; that, as Justice Holmes put it, the mode by which the inevitable came to pass was effort; that to perpetrate a harm was always wrong no matter how many joined in it but to perpetrate it on a weaker person or people was particularly detestable; and so on.

Idle Thoughts

Our institutions are founded on the assumption that most people follow these principles most of the time because they want to, and the institutions work pretty well when this assumption is true. More recently, however, bright people have been fooling with the machinery in the human head and they have discovered quite a lot. For instance, we know that association and repetition play a large part in the implanting of ideas. This has unexpected results. We no longer engage in the arduous task of making a better mousetrap to induce the world to beat a path to our door. We associate with our product a comely and exposed damsel, or a continued story which speeds daily through the air rejected only by the ionosphere.

So far the matter does not seem too serious. But when Hitler introduced new refinements they were serious. It appears to be true that people can be united most quickly by hatred of a comparatively weak group in the community and by the common sense of guilt that accompanies outrages against its members. We have had some experience of this ourselves. With this as a start and all the perverted ingenuity of propaganda, which uses familiar and respected words and ideas to implant the exact opposite standard and goal, a whole people have been utterly confused and corrupted. Unhappily neither the possession of this knowledge nor the desire to use it was confined to Hitler.

Others dip from this same devil's cauldron. The politician who knows that notoriety survives the context is anxious to be mentioned as often as possible.

The perfect tool at hand is controversy. For controversy is far more diverting than exposition, and, therefore, the press and radio are more than willing to assist. They have been known to pitch some balls of their own. And no controversy is safer than one with the foreigner, the outsider. His defenders at once become suspect. So a field which is difficult enough, where more than anywhere widespread agreement is essential, becomes a peculiar prey to controversy.

There is also the new psychology of crisis—exemplified by the common expression, "to build a fire under him." Now in my archaic profession to do that is to commit arson; and the law takes a dim view of it. But abroad and at home it has been observed that to obtain relief from the unendurable produces a quite irrational sense of well-being. Therefore, the unendurable situation is created so that one may profit from the circumstances of relief.

It is, I believe, a Russian fable which recounts the advice given by a priest to a peasant who insisted that he was about to commit suicide because his life was so unbearable. The advice was for a week to move his goats and chickens into his own hut, and then to move them out. The advice, of course, was sound. Life took on a definitely rosier hue and the idea of suicide was abandoned. It is not recommended as a sound practice, like swinging two bats before going to the plate.

The evil is not merely that the perpetrator of the crisis misjudges his own skill and involves us all in disaster, but that, as with all these practices, a Gresham's law of politics and morals sets in. The baser practice drives out the better. The cheaper, the more fantastic, the more adapted to prejudice, the more reckless the appeal or the maneuver, the more attention, and excited attention, it receives. And the less chance there is that we shall listen to the often difficult analysis of the facts and the always difficult consideration of duty.

It is evil for shrewd men to play on the minds and loyalties and fears of their fellows as on an instrument. It produces not only the degradation of the democratic dogma about which Brooks Adams warned, but the degradation of all mankind everywhere, paralyzing the very centers of moral action, until these oceans of cunning words wash through the minds of men like the sea through the empty portholes of a derelict.

If the need for a remedy seems urgent, it might be sought both through attaining an intellectual immunity to this virus by identifying and isolating it and also by making it plain to its carriers at home and abroad by the plainest words and acts that they are not fit company for morally healthy people.

These practices, I said a moment ago, seemed to me a contributing factor in the trouble we have in focusing the will of people on problems beyond our shores. Perhaps, even more than this, they have contributed to those problems. If it is true, as I believe it is, that the continued moral, military, and economic power of the United States is an essential factor in the organization of peace, then these matters about which we have been talking have greatly contributed to our troubles. They lie at the root of the hysteria which has wrought such havoc with our armed services, and continues to do so. They lie at the root, also, of the difficulty which we have in using our great economic power, in our own interest, to hasten recovery in other countries along lines which are essential to our own system. They have contributed largely to the weakening of our economic strength itself. The slogans, "Bring the Boys Home!" and "Don't Be Santa Claus!" are not among our more gifted or thoughtful contributions to the creation of a free and tranquil world.

This seems to me true for the simplest of all reasons, which is that the sensible way to strengthen a structure is not to weaken its most essential parts. I am often told that the way to solve this or that problem is to leave it to the United Nations. But it seems to me inescapable that if they are, or we hope they will be, united, they are still nations; and no more can be expected of this forum for political adjustment than the sum total of the contributions. If these are wise and steadfast and supported by strength determined to organize peace, the results will be good. But, in the Arab proverb, the ass that went to Mecca remained an ass, and a policy has little added to it by its place of utterance.

So, when one sees our military forces disrupted, one is entitled to ask whether the considerations which led to this were more valid and urgent than the sense of steadiness and confidence which our forces gave and would have continued to give to millions all

Idle Thoughts

over a badly shattered and uncertain world. The answer which one most often gets does not go to the merits of the question. It goes to another of our devices for finding out what we think—opinion polls. It appears that we have become extroverts, if of a somewhat hypochondriac type, and ascertain our state of health by this mass temperature taking. Fortunately this was not one of the hardships of Valley Forge.

So, too, those who must labor daily at the crossings where the lives of many people meet understand better than they can expound that their tasks can be lightened but not performed by a resolution drafted and passed at the United Nations. These tasks are more deeply affected by how we and others master the intricacies of the production and movement of food and other goods, with how successfully we deal with labor problems and inflation, with credits, with the wise use of natural resources. They even involve the most national of all problems—the efficiency of the administrative and legislative processes.

At this point I am aware of voices which say that national sovereignty is the root of the whole trouble and that we must do away with all of that. It may be so, but to a sinking heart there comes the admonition of Old Hickory at the battle of New Orleans, apocryphally reported by Paul Porter—"Boys, elevate them guns a little lower." It may be that the way to solve a difficult problem is to transfer one's attention to an insoluble one. But I doubt it.

Rather it seems to me the path of hope is toward the concrete, toward the manageable, in the first instance. A forum there should be, and there is, for the adjustment, as best we can, of those critical issues which threaten the peace. But, when we come to tasks of common management, it seems wise to start with those which through hard and intelligent work can be reduced to manageable dimensions and governed by pretty specific rules and standards—like the monetary fund, the bank, the trade organization, and, if possible, the control of atomic energy. These are hard enough in all conscience. I have chewed on them and know their toughness and the frailty of the task forces and their plans. But the jobs are doable with good sense and good luck.

To do these jobs and conduct our own affairs with passable restraint and judgment—the type of judgment, as Justice Brandeis used to say, which leads a man not to stand in front of a locomotive—will be an achievement. Moreover, it will be an achievement which will profoundly modify many situations which now concern us, including—and I am now guessing—our relations with the Soviet Union. Problems which are difficult against a background of confusion, hesitation, and disintegration may well become quite possible of solution as national and international institutions and activities become healthy and confident and vigorous in a large part of the world. Certainly our troubles would not increase.

But it is a long and tough job and one for which we as a people are not particularly suited. We believe that any problem can be solved with a little ingenuity and without inconvenience to the folks at large. We have trouble-shooters to do this. And our name for problems is significant. We call them headaches. You take a powder and they are gone. These pains about which we have been talking are not like that. They are like the pain of earning a living. They will stay with us until death. We have got to understand that all our lives the danger, the uncertainty, the need for alertness, for effort, for discipline will be upon us. This is new to us. It will be hard for us. But we are in for it and the only real question is whether we shall know it soon enough.

Culture after Breakfast

In the years when I had some connection with the United States Information Service and the Voice of America I heard a good deal about American culture—from those who contributed to it, those who absorbed it, those who dispensed it, and from the Congress, which took a very dark view of it in any form. Only recently I have had a new view from a young colleague who had just toured South Asia, the Soviet Union, and the Eastern European satellites. Whatever, he reported, might be said about American foreign policy—and a good deal was said—American jazz reigned unchallenged from Bombay through Tashkent, Moscow to Warsaw and Belgrade. "How," he asked a Pole, "can you listen to this stuff?" "Ah!" said the Pole, "You ought to hear what we have had to hear for years!" Well, I thought, what gurgles like

The Reporter, September 19, 1957.

Idle Thoughts

water in a weary land is worth a taste.

But the example of the Poles, alone, would not have been enough to make me switch on the radio in the morning. An occasional concert in the evening, yes; but after breakfast, never. What finally turned the trick was boredom. For years the summer morning drive from our Maryland farm to Washington was a joy of fresh, clean day before the sullen heat had spoiled it. But now only the first few miles are that— the red-wing blackbirds and meadowlarks along the honeysuckled fences, the wood doves here and there on a telephone wire, the mockingbirds with their aristocratic drawling flight, and their wings left open for an instant after alighting, like an eighteenth-century Corinthian about to raise his quizzing glass, cattle still eager for the damp grass, and my friend, the nurseryman, cultivating between his rows of box rootings. This soon ends as our rolling and twisting country road drains into the eight-lane divided highway and one development merges into another, each announcing itself as such-and-such gardens, hills, knolls, valley, or arcadia. That is when I push the first radio station button and begin to learn again what has grown dim since last year.

A female voice greets me, singing, with depressing vivacity, "The most beautiful thing in Silver Spring is a Loving Chevrolet." Surrounded by this sprawling young metropolis—the second city of Maryland—flowing over farms, woods, and streams like lava from an urban Vesuvius, one acknowledges that she may well be right. And then the mind drifts off to wonder whether a Chevrolet really could be loving. I once had an open, blue Chrysler with wings on the radiator cap which definitely was. But the music cuts off reverie.

There is something unique and categoric about all music played from, say, eight-thirty to ten o'clock in the morning. No doubt about it, something turns the morning disc jockey to thoughts of love. All the other great subjects of song from the earliest ballad and Icelandic saga down don't add up to two per cent of the time. War songs, marching songs, patriotic songs, drinking songs, songs of old times, songs of laughter, songs of lament, lullabies, mother and home songs—they can't hold a candle to love. It seems a little like ending breakfast with a stiff bourbon. But, then, I once knew a Swedish entomologist who fortified himself for his morning with his net on beer, pickled herring, and goat's cheese. It's all in what one is used to.

But love songs, as sung over the morning radio, are quite a bit more varied in mood than one might imagine. In general, they are keyed down, a sound concession to the hour so difficult for those whose zest for life gathers momentum slowly. Of this genre is the philosophical love song. The writer of one of these songs clearly was entrapped by the dilemma posed by Bishop Berkeley regarding the nature of reality. Can, for instance, a rose blush unseen when color is the effect produced on the retina of the eye by an object? This writer crashes right into the whole tangled issue and becomes lyrical about whether he loves his inamorata because she is beautiful, or whether she seems to him to be beautiful because he loves her. Well there you are. In my view, it's anyone's guess, though it might be a help to have a look at the girl before guessing. But my real puzzlement is over what difference it makes to him practically. Then, too, he ought to look at it from the girl's point of view.

Another type is the materialistic song, the one which believes that love can be bought. In one of these the troubadour promises to buy his lady a rainbow, and then in a burst of reckless extravagance throws in the moon, too. I am dead against this sort of idea being put in girls' heads. Some woman probably wrote it. It can lead to no end of trouble and might undermine the home.

"A Teenager's Romance" looks at the matter from a new and somewhat arresting point of view. To him, so he sings, love is only another facet of an old problem—his elders. This time the old spoilsports, who appear under the incognito of "they," have apparently insisted that the young Romeo and Juliet are not to be relied upon, as it is euphemistically put, to tell black from white. At first glance, "they" would seem to have something of a point, as the old man is probably trying to get him at least through high school unencumbered. Then one wonders how good, on the record, "they" are at telling black from white themselves. Most arguments between adults end by each telling the other that he is unable to do just that.

In the world of song "they" is a sinister concept. They can't take away the sunset, they can't take away the moon. "They" is what makes a man sorry for himself and usually is himself.

The songs in which love poses an unusual, and often unique, problem have a special interest for me. One never knows how they are coming out. I have two in mind, one sung by a man, one by a woman. The man's song is called "It's Not for Me to Say." The title suggests a wide field, but what he picks out as not for him to say seems very odd indeed—it is that his girl loves him. This seems so reasonable a proposition that one wonders what bothers him. He goes on to explain. All he has to go on, he says, is hope, as he holds her in his arms and presses his lips to hers, that perhaps day by day this may blossom into love. But if this is not to be and if fate sends them on their separate ways never to meet again, it has all been worthwhile. This man takes whatever the future may bring without flinching.

The girl has a different problem. She warns not to be misled by the cold gleam in her eye because down below the flames in her heart fairly roar—so much so, in fact, that she suggests alerting the fire department before the next meeting. A very fair girl, a little aghast at her own potential, greatly to be commended for giving a man a break by posting the notice—"Road open. Proceed at your own risk."

This bring us to the last, and proportionately much the largest, category—songs of unrequited love. The early-morning troubadours can't resist these. They begin with the revived and much-sung favorite entitled "I'm Gonna Sit Right Down and Write Myself a Letter." Conduct, otherwise incomprehensible, is ex-

Idle Thoughts

plained by a lady so indifferent that the postman doesn't even ring once. This pathetic case is followed by "Love Letters in the Sand" whose depressing message needs no elaboration, though, of course, "aches" and "breaks" furnish needed rhymes throughout. My son tells me of the acme of defeat in love that used to come over the radio to the men in the Pacific during the war, perhaps sung by Tokyo Rose, containing the morale-building thought that the singer was born to lose and now was losing her. In "Dark Moon" unrequited love goes into an astronomical phase. Why, the moon is asked, is its splendor gone; and the anthropomorphic suggestion is advanced that perhaps it shares the sorrow of a lost love. The moon is too much of a lady to reply that she is at her darkest just before the new moon.

As a final note of hope among the ruins is "Love in the Afternoon." Are its title and thought perhaps a little reminiscent of Hemingway? At any rate, it brings to those who see the shadows lengthen the hope that between them and the chill of evening there may still be Something.

As I turn into the garage and switch off the radio, I ponder the observation of Andrew Fletcher of Saltoun that if a man could write the songs of a nation, he need not care who should make the laws. Is it possible that between legislators and minstrels the score at the bottom of the ninth is nothing to nothing, with two out and no hits?

Toast at the Oxford-Cambridge Boat Race Dinner

Memories of rowing go back through the past eternity of my life to its early days. The joy of those late spring afternoons is still as fresh as ever it was, far out on New Haven harbor or on the Thames above Gales Ferry and after the wind had dropped and the crew had worked itself into perfect harmony and rhythm. One concentrated without thought on the sweaty back before one, felt the lift as oars bit into water and flashed out again for the long, smooth run of the shell between strokes. Even the coach's megaphone would be silent and only the coxswain, barking the stroke, broke the afternoon silence. One found then an answer to the prayer of the collect: "May our hearts surely there be fixed where true joys are to be found."

Delivered in Washington, D.C., April 3, 1954.

33

Idle Thoughts

The figure in the coach's launch, not as well known then as it has since become, had been a familiar of school and college in what might be termed the field of our major scholastic concentration—rowing and all that pertained thereto. Yale in those days had been seduced by the chief tenet of English rowing—amateur coaching. To adopt it at New Haven, Mr. W. Averell Harriman and I in the summer of 1913 had gone to Henley-on-Thames with our visiting English coaches to learn what we could, first at Henley and then at Oxford, about English rowing, shells, and coaching.

One of the English maxims of those days was that the way to learn to race was to race. This made up in terseness and epigrammatic quality what it lacked in completeness of analysis. But we liked it, and on our return arranged a fall race with Princeton on Lake Carnegie. Well, we had it—in all senses of the word. At least, it could be called a race in a sort of generic way, though we never were close enough to Princeton to permit general conversation between the boats.

We were not disturbed and felt that all concerned had learned much. Not so the Yale rowing committee, presided over by a former Yale Crew captain, then a partner in Morgan and Co. The evening of the race the rowing committee met. On Monday morning all connection between Messrs. Harriman and Acheson and Yale rowing rested solely in memory.

This was my first experience of being fired. Since then more illustrious authority has performed the rite. I am wholly familiar with the suggestion that it was widely desired. But I have never been in better company. From this experience I learned two comforting truths. One was that the sweetest way of being relieved of responsibility without self-reproach is to be unjustly fired; the other, that the University had other resources than the boathouse and that the mind was quite as interesting as a sliding seat.

This thought brings me appreciably closer to the business at hand, by way of some discourse on the subject of the purpose of a university. It may surprise you to learn that there was a time when men seemed to be clear about this; for instance, the founders of my own university at New Haven. The first paragraph of the "Act for Liberty to erect a Collegiate School" in 1701 recites:

> Whereas several well disposed and Publick spirited Persons of their sincere Regard to & Zeal for upholding & Propagating of the Christian Protestant Religion by a succession of Learned & Orthodox men have expressed by Petition their earnest desires that full Liberty and Priveledge be granted unto Certain Undertakers for the founding, suitably endowing & ordering a Collegiate School within his Maj^ties Colony of Connecticot wherein Youth may be instructed in the Arts & Sciences who thorough the blessing of Almighty God may be fitted for Publick employment both in Church & Civil State.

Here was the purpose—as clear as a bell—the fitting for Publick employment both in Church and Civil State.

Idle Thoughts

The high, though discreet, place of learning in this endeavor is shown by Article 23 of the bylaws, with its inflexible determination to maintain standards.

> The degree of Master of Arts [it provides] shall be conferred *ex officio* and without public presentation, upon any person who is elected a member of the Corporation or who is a Professor in the University and who has not already received its master's or doctor's degree.

They should, at least, have the appearance of learning.

Emerson, alas, having attended instruction at another place, received an unfavorable opinion of its results, certainly in fitting youth for employment in Civil State.

> We are students of words [he wrote]. We are shut up in schools and colleges and recitation rooms for ten or fifteen years, and come out at last with a bag of wind, a memory of words, and do not know a thing.

This I often think is too sweeping. Many of our public men seem to me disciples of the Aristotelian doctrine that every block of marble contains a statue —when the superfluous parts are chipped away. There is, to be sure, a problem here as to what parts are superfluous, and this often becomes trying when the work is done by a number of sculptors, such as a "team" or "task force."

How well the universities which have hatched the

Oxford-Cambridge Boat Race Dinner

distinguished clutch of eggheads present here this evening did their work only you would know, though the presence of so many and so distinguished representatives of journalism and diplomacy permits deductions. My own knowledge is far less than yours, for the very reason which in a way makes my relation to the Universities more agreeable—as unearned rewards are always sweeter than those which are merely one's just due.

But this relation by adoption, and the newness of it, has one disability. It leaves lacking the true spirit of partisanship which is needed to flavor a speech on this occasion. I remind myself, almost but not quite, of Alben Barkley's Kentuckian who, when asked about his stand on two rival candidates, said, "I haven't made up my mind yet; but when I do, I'll be bitter as hell." Indeed, I can feel the beginnings of bitterness at Dr. Trapp's lines, when in 1715 King George the First sent troops to Oxford and gave Bishop Ely's library to Cambridge.

> The King, observing with judicious eyes
> The state of both his universities,
> To Oxford sent a troop of horse, and why?
> That learned body wanted loyalty;
> To Cambridge books, as very well discerning
> How much that loyal body wanted learning.

At once the hackles rise at the effrontery of one who would hold loyalty hearings at Oxford or impugn the erudition of Cambridge.

Idle Thoughts

So with malice toward neither, with charity, respect, honor, and affection toward both, I propose a toast to the Universities of Oxford and Cambridge.

Part Two ⋘

Stories

Of Mice and Mail

Long ago, when the world was young, the official censor of English usage and prose style in the Department of State was a charming lady with an imposing and elegant coiffure. In those days we were in the old State, War, and Navy Building, just west of the White House. Affection for its tiers of pillared balconies and mansard roof and its present mantle of soft dove gray is the touchstone which separates aging Victorian aesthetes from neoclassicists and moderns. We loved, also, its swinging, slatted, saloon-type half doors. They not only provided ventilation before air conditioning and permitted most covenants to be overheard and hence openly arrived at, but their vicious swings into the hall created a sporting hazard for passersby.

The Department was much smaller then. The

The Atlantic Monthly, March, 1965.

country had not yet reluctantly donned the imperial purple of world leadership, or acquired a voice heard hourly around the world, or discovered and exchanged culture; nor was it required to cope with the mounting ill will of the objects of its solicitude and generosity. The days when the Department would add to its little nucleus of diplomatists the equivalent of Montgomery Ward, Chautauqua, CBS, and Lincoln Center were still mercifully ahead.

So much smaller was it that at the end of the day the elegantly coiffured chieftainess of the Division of Coordination and Review could and did bring to my office all the important departmental mail, to be read and signed over the title Acting Secretary. We began with a ritual which would have puzzled the uninitiated. She pulled a chair close to the front of my desk and then sat, not on it, but in it—that is, she perched herself cross-legged in the chair. And thereby hangs a tale.

The Undersecretary's mouse lived in his office fireplace, where for years a wood fire had been laid but never touched, much less lighted. Probably generations of internationally minded mice had grown up within the log structure and gone on to positions in the United Nations. When the long day's work was ending and the busy office was hushed and the fever of departmental life was over, the mouse would come out. Some atavistic fear or urge, older than time, leads women to slander mice by believing that they harbor a lascivious desire to run up the female leg. Elephants seem to share this fear. At any rate, both are traditionally nervous in the presence of mice.

From her safe haven the chieftainess could observe the mouse without tremors as we tackled the mail. For years she had battled bravely with the bureaucracy and maintained the State Department's standard of literacy high above that, for instance, of the Department of Agriculture or the Bureau of Internal Revenue. But time had damped her fire and dulled her cutting edge. She welcomed the help of fresh enthusiasm and a new blade.

We won a few opening and easy victories over phrases with no solid support—villainous expressions like "as regards to," "acknowledging yours of," "regretting our delay in," and so on. Then came our first major attack on a departmental favorite. The target was the use of the verb "to feel" to describe the Department's cogitating and deciding process. "The Department feels that to adopt the course you urge would not," et cetera, et cetera. The Department could, I insisted, decide, agree, disagree, approve, disapprove, conclude, and on rare occasions, and vicariously, think, but never feel. It had no feelings. It was incapable of feeling. So the ukase was issued that departmental feeling was out.

The immediacy of our success brought home to us the immensity of our combined power over the written words. When the chieftainess eliminated feeling from every letter no matter by whom written and I signed letters brought to me only by her, the Department simply ceased to feel. Absolute power, Lord Acton wrote, corrupts absolutely. But in our case, it was not so. Moderation was our guide. The tumbrel was filled discriminately. Into it went "implement" and "contact" used as verbs—"the Department must implement the Act of Congress" or "you should contact the Consul General at Antwerp." These horrors sneezed into the sack. So did "finalize," "analogize," and "flexible" when used to modify "approach." "To trigger" would have done so likewise if anyone had dared use it.

Thus far the natives showed no signs of restlessness under the new order. Indeed, they hardly noticed the increased literacy and clarity of their returning carbon copies. But our pruning knives soon cut deeper into clichés which had taken the place of thought. The first of these was "contraproductive." What would a congressman think, I asked, when he read, "The course you propose would, in the Department's view, prove to be contraproductive"? It would sound to him suspiciously like a veiled reference to birth control.

Once started on this line of thought, we soon added to the proscribed list two other phrases, also likely to suggest undue familiarity with the shady side of sex. These were "abortive attempts" and "emasculating amendments." "Crippling" amendments were bad enough. Why not, in both cases, switch to "stultifying" for a change?

Even these oddities were put down to no more than reluctance to admit modern ruggedness of speech into official correspondence. But when the guns were turned on "sincere," the murmurs grew. "For proof of Russian sincerity," someone would write, "we look to deeds not words." Nothing could have been more misleading or misinformed concerning both the meaning of the word and the nature of the Russians. Under pressure all would agree that Webster relegated to fifth place the letter writer's belief that "sincere" meant "virtuous." As its first meaning, Noah put down just what the Russians were: "pure; unmixed; unadulterated; as, sincere milk," or, one might add, as sincere—that is, unmixed and unadulterated—trouble. He even quoted the eighteenth-century wit, physician, and friend of Pope and Swift, John Arbuthnot, as writing incomprehensibly), "There is no sincere acid in any animal juice." That clinched the matter, and "sincere" as an adjectival encomium went on the *Index Prohibitorum.*

We were tempted to go further and rule out "Sincerely yours," either as a self-serving declaration that the Department was "unmixed," which was false on its face, or that, taking a lower meaning, it was "without deceit," which the body of the letter usually disproved. We preferred "Respectfully yours" for our superiors in the White House and the Capitol, a reserved "Very truly yours" for the citizenry, and for foreign VIP's, the stately "With renewed expressions of my highest esteem" (a delightful phrase, since the expressions were never expressed). But "Sincerely yours," having by usage been deprived of all meaning, was finally adjudged suitable for departmental use.

Thus we strove mightily at the noble task of returning the Department's prose to a Jeffersonian level; but we strove against the current. We became obstacles to efficiency. The mail backed up. Congressmen complained of the delay in answering their letters and refused to be assuaged by the superior prose of the answers when they did come.

When the first symptoms of elephantiasis appeared with our absorption of Colonel Donovan's Research and Intelligence people and Elmer Davis's foreign-broadcasting facilities, our doom was sealed. Our evening sessions with the mail became as hopelessly inadequate as Gandhi's spinning wheel. The revolution of expansion swept our ukases away, and through the ruins the exiled phrases defiantly marched back, contacting, implementing, feeling, contraproducing, aborting, and emasculating in shameless abandon.

The Great Fish of Como

A westering October sun fell on the mountainside across the lake, flashing on the windows of the yellow stucco houses which climbed steeply up its side. But already Cernobbio and the lake before it lay in shadow. Soon a chill mist would come off the water. The fishermen sitting motionless and neatly spaced along the lake wall would take in their lines and wander off. They were in no hurry, for they were contemplative fishermen whose ambitions did not lie in the restless world of action. Their predecessors had sat along that wall since before Caesar's legions had trudged northward past the lake to man the passes in Helvetia and to push on into Gaul, lying beyond and divided into three parts.

For centuries Como fishermen had been fishermen by faith and for the joy of a composed spirit, not for

Harper's, June, 1959.

47

the joy of battle. Their fish were the fish of faith—things believed in not seen, and given just a glimmer of reality by gentle tuggings from the murky depths and by the occasional loss of bait. They asked little, these fishermen, and received little—little, that is, in the way of fish. Other bounties were heaped upon them, the warmth of the sun, the endlessly changing beauty of the lake, and the pageant of its busy life. These were reward enough for sensible men.

My companion had gone off to paint, leaving me to a pleasantly aimless walk along the shore road toward the town of Como. At first, this had its distractions, even alarms; but it became clear that the motor bus, car, scooter, and bicycle operators did not really intend to run me down, and that they lost interest if one showed complete indifference. Soon I found myself absorbed in the fishermen, soothed by their still composure into opening my heart to the beauty around me and to the gentle joy of being alive. I was as wholly unprepared for—indeed, undesirous of—action and effort as the fisherman himself.

He was either a man of imagination or something of a recluse; for he had deserted the even sequence of lake-wall sitters and gone out on a stone jetty which made an incomplete semi-circle from the wall, leaving at its other end an opening just wide enough to let small craft find shelter in its minute harbor. Here stood the fisherman near the open end of the jetty, fishing on the lake side, alone, with his back to the traffic thirty yards away, not sitting like the others, but yet not tense. He seemed like a man about to understand something, as though he might be about to say for the first time, "I will lift up mine eyes unto the hills."

Then it happened—just as I came abreast of him and was about to go by. His rod bent sharply and jerked violently. Whatever he was about to think left him. He became all action, mixed with cunning and caution. I stopped, frozen to the spot with excitement. Was it only an old tire he had hooked onto? Or was it, could it possibly be, that so much faith exercised for so long had had its effect, had, perhaps, even created a fish? The surface broke into flying spray and for a second a tail—it seemed as big as a mermaid's tail— appeared. Then the rod bent again, even further, and the struggle was on.

My lungs were nearly bursting with holding my breath. Out it all went in the one word of Italian of which I was sure.

"Bravo!" I shouted.

All the fishermen turned their heads some to right, some to left, but they did not move. Other men, however, truer simians, gave in to curiosity; and, then, to excitement. A few bicyclists stopped and joined me; then some scooters; then a car. This blocked the lake side of the road. Along came a bus, was unable to get through, so passengers and driver got out to watch. No one honked. No one had any engagement any more important than to watch the miracle occurring in the lake.

Stories

The battle waxed and waned. At times, water flew in floppings and splashings. At times, the fish made long runs out into the lake. Both brought cheering and shouted encouragement in Italian more versatile than mine. But I was glad to notice that my "Bravo" was pretty generally approved and accepted as just the word for these tense moments. The crowd grew. A policeman joined us from headquarters about a block away.

At other times the fish would sound and sulk along the bottom. This gave all of us the deepest concern, and we shouted our worry about the state of affairs. The fisherman answered in pantomime, pretending inability to lift a massive weight.

The battle seemed a long one, so great was our tension. But, of course, it was not, and soon the spent fish was clearly to be seen close to the surface, all fight gone out of him (I never thought of it as "her"). All that remained was to land the prize. All were guessing its weight, some pretty optimistically. My own guess was about two and a half or three pounds, species unknown, a good fish anywhere.

Suddenly one could almost feel the freezing horror of the thought which struck us all at the same time, including the fisherman. All that remained was to land the prize. But land him how? The fisherman was on top of the jetty. The fish was ten feet below in the water. The jetty was smooth and sheer, the best Italian masonry. The water was cold and deep. Cries of despair and commiseration mingled with the deepening shadows.

The Great Fish of Como

The shouting stopped as the fisherman began to move. He had a plan. Our questioning murmurs followed him as he led the fish along the jetty to the harbor opening, and into it. Further and further into the harbor he went, until, in a flash, the plan was revealed. Halfway along the jetty a flight of stone steps led down to the boat landing, and that was where the fisherman was leading the fish. Again the twilight quiet was shattered by acclaim. As Macaulay might have put it, "Even the ranks of Tuscany could scarce forbear to cheer." A resourceful man, this fisherman of ours. We found ourselves shaking hands in the crowd. The man who left now, or honked his horn, was no man at all.

Down the steps, almost on tiptoe and with great caution, came the fisherman to meet the fish in the tense moment of the coup de grâce. But, as he came down from the wall, he got no nearer to the fish, which seemed to go farther out in the water. We shouted our puzzled questions; again the answer came in pantomime. The fisherman had no reel. His line was tied to the end of a bamboo pole. High as he held the pole, the line was too long to come within his grasp. He did not dare relax the tension on the line for fear the hook might come loose. Again, despair!

But, again, he had a plan, though this time not even the wisest or most imaginative observer could guess it. Up the steps he went and along the jetty to where he had started. The fish followed docilely below. Fumbling among the scraggly weeds he produced—of all things—an umbrella. Then along the jetty, again, and down the steps. We watched in silent bewilderment.

On the boat landing, with the pole in his left hand, he deftly opened the umbrella with his right by a quick jerk. Then he began to maneuver the fish inshore. The plan was unfolded as sheer genius. The umbrella was to be a landing net.

Again cheers, cheers of hope and expectation. But the fish ceased to co-operate. Tired though it was, the umbrella, held menacingly out, frightened it; and the umbrella was unwieldly. Twice the fish was led within umbrella reach, but eluded the pass. Each time the crowd drew in its breath, held it, and let it out as a sigh.

The third time, the plan worked. Up came the umbrella, water pouring from a hundred holes, but with the fish flopping lustily inside.

A cheer half-uttered died as we realized that the outcome would be a close thing. Here, if ever, was the time for resolution. But it was just here that the fisherman's resolution wavered. He had met every challenge with resourceful action. But that spouting, ungainly umbrella wetting his feet and trousers, that rejuvenated fish splashing water in his face with its hysterical floppings bewildered him and rattled him. A determined rush away from the water and a wet closing of the umbrella on the fish, and all would be over. But he hesitated. The fish was held up by the stays of the umbrella dangerously near its edge. Each flop brought it above the edge. At the first one, out flew the hook. But the breathtaking issue was would the fish fall back in the umbrella, or into the water? Warnings died in our throats. The man was rattled enough.

The fish gave a tremendous flop. Up it went, cleared the umbrella's rim, and fell back into the water. For a moment it hardly moved. Then slowly, drunkenly, sometimes almost on its side, it disappeared in the murky water.

No one moved. The fisherman stared for a moment at the spot where the fish had been, then looked up at us ranged along the lake wall above him. A half smile broke across his face and slowly he raised his shoulders and his hands with the palms up in one all-encompassing shrug. "Such is life." "After all it is only a game." "Well, I'll be damned." All this the gesture said. But it conveyed puzzlement, too. Had there been a fish at all? Or had a contemplative fisherman, a fisherman by faith alone, been tempted into the world of action, only to be taught that there no true joys were to be found? That was it; there had been no fish.

Motors coughed and raced; bicyclists shoved off; the passengers made a rush for the bus. I turned back toward Cernobbio in the deepening dusk. Northward above the lake a star lighted; and then another. Not a fisherman was in sight. Had there, I wondered, been any?

The Greeks Come to the Isola

"It would be best," said the concierge, "to make a reservation. Tomorrow is Sunday and many people may wish to go to the *isola*."

"But," I protested, "if many people wish to go on Sunday, *I* do *not* wish to go. I will go on Monday."

This childishness he smiled aside, tolerant, gentle, and unmoved. "It is best," he said, "to make a reservation. Many people is not too many people. For Sunday at one o'clock."

"For four," I added meekly.

"For four—Sunday at one. The launch will be waiting at eleven." He wrote it all down as he spoke; and that was settled.

On Sunday morning the launch was waiting at the stone steps at the Villa d'Este, made fast, bow and stern, to wooden piles gay in their red and yellow corkscrew stripes. A touch of gaiety was not a bad thing, I thought, as I handed my companion down the steps to the boatman, who stood steadying the craft, holding an umbrella against a rain squall and offering a hand to the lady with solemn and imperturbable courtesy.

"*E nulla, Signora,*" he murmured, waving aside the low scudding clouds which shut off the opposite shore; then, closing us in the minute cabin, he shoved off. His confidence was contagious. Though he sat in the open, driving the launch into a blinding squall with the rain running off his cap and ears down his neck, yet we knew that the course was set for luncheon for four on the terrace of the *isola*.

And so it was. In the short hour's run up the lake to pick up our friends, the sun was out, tearing the clouds apart; and Italy was looking as only Italy, drying her eyes, can look. Our friends were waving on the quay. In a moment they were aboard; the top of the cabin was rolled back; we headed for our island, while the boatman steamed gently in the October sun.

"It was there," said our friend, pointing, "right beside that white church halfway up the hill that Mussolini and his mistress were shot." The sun lost its warmth. *That* world had no place in this Sunday morning. No one spoke. Then everyone did; but not about the white church halfway up the hill. In a moment we had rounded a point and it was lost to sight.

Stories

Our friends had bought a villa just where the lake divides. When we had visited them there, our car wound up a steep road built for donkeys and cattle to a village of stone and stucco. In its center the road widened a bit before an arched carriage entrance on the left, set in solid masonry and closed by massive wooden doors. At the sound of our horn they had swung wide to let us into what had been the stable and now opened onto a colonnade along the front of the house. Emerging from its cool dimness, we had caught our breath.

Far below, beyond the treetops and roofs along the terraces through which we had climbed, lay the lake, flashing back the dazzling sunlight with, here and there, dark shadows on its surface from the few clouds still left. We stood there looking.

"Do you ever become so used to this that you look without seeing?" I asked.

"No," she said, "never. But still I like to go down the hill, because coming back this first look always stops me here, as though I had never seen it before."

The villa was stone even to its marble floors and stairs, the new part eighteenth-century, the rest centuries older. No one knew when the terrace garden with its exotic trees and shrubs had been laid out. The gardener had cared for it all his life. When the former owner died, he readily got another job but asked to be allowed to stay on with his family over the stable, so that he could tend his beloved garden until someone else came to do it. Now he was back full-time, ecstatically happy, and teaching his son how to work with the earth and nature.

When my host told me this, it had brought back a re-mark of G. M. Young's:[1] That people thought of statesmen as architects drawing on blank sheets plans for structures to be; but in fact they should be thought of as gardeners who must work with the earth as they find it and for whom achievement could come only by understanding and using the eternal processes of nature.

How would it be, I wondered, if there were fewer lawyers and more gardeners in public life? Then I recalled that our host was a banker, turned diplomat, a rare combination, I used to tell him, of cold-blooded calculation. Would a gardener be a match for him in negotiation? Or for an ex-coal miner turned dicta-tor? Perhaps lawyers had their usefulness, after all.

To make talk while thoughts of the white church faded, I said, "You are good to leave your beautiful villa and try a Sunday lunch at the island. I hope it is not crowded. The hotel has made a reservation."

Our guest had never been there, she said, but she had heard that it was pleasant at the island and that one had a good meal. The boatman, who had been standing well offshore, turned into a strait about a hundred yards wide between a small island and the shore. Then he cut the motor and drifted in for a landing.

A raft made of a few logs with slats across them

1. G. M. Young, *Stanley Baldwin* (London: Rupert Hart-Davis, 1952), p. 132.

connected by a plank with the shore. Its buoyancy was low. To stand on it to help the ladies ashore would land them in ankle-deep water. So it became each woman for herself, with rescue waiting on the bank. Then a slow climb up the stone steps cut around the cliff to the restaurant forty feet above.

We heard the chatter and laughter before our heads rose above the brick floor of the terrace. Some fifteen tables seating from two to eight—mostly families with children, a few lovers, all Italian—were scattered about up to the low wall beyond which lay the lake. There was no empty table. A few trees threw spotty shade. On a path leading to a slightly higher grassy knoll a few more people sauntered; dogs barked at one another; children chased the dogs. The laughter seemed directed toward a large man standing in the center of the terrace. As we gained the level he turned and greeted us.

Here, one knew at once, was a notable character. He had the look of a paunchy satyr, blended with that of a middle-aged Dionysus without the beard. Black hair, curly and long, was thinning on top and receding. His eyes squinted in quizzical amusement. A long nose for knowing, and white teeth for smiling, were set in a plump (but not fat) South Italian face. His sports shirt opened at the neck, revealing a black bushiness; an embroidered Greek waistcoat with brass buttons hung unbuttoned. Around his paunch was tied a red-and-white checked tablecloth, below which protruded black pantaloons and bare feet in wooden clogs.

The Greeks Come to the *Isola*

"A table," said our guest in Italian, looking about doubtfully, "was reserved for the *signore*." This produced a half-subdued roar from the proprietor.

"Ah, *Signora*, all one need do is to take a sensible man, dress him up like a drum major, make a concierge of him, and he becomes all puffed up and makes a great fuss about nothing. A reservation, is it? Who wants reservations? You shall have your table, the best."

He walked over to a shed by the side of a long, low, red-tiled brick building—which was evidently restaurant, kitchen, and house all in one—threw back a tarpaulin, and produced with a flourish a round wicker table in one hand and two chairs in the other. A shout produced a small replica of the proprietor, with a smaller tablecloth about his smaller waist, who brought two more chairs and a red-and-white checked tablecloth.

"Your table, *Signore, Signori*." He bowed us to our places and had the table set almost as we sat down. At this point my companion took charge of matters. She is a lady of sophistication, who knows her way about, and could see that this sort of thing, all very well within limits, could get out of hand and was already amusing our fellow lunchers. With that touch on the reins and tone of voice which has told many a spirited horse and some other mammals who was in command, she said, "May we have menus, please?"

For a moment not a sound, not a movement came from Dionysus. Then through the amazement registered on that mobile face dawned sympathetic understanding merging into the solemn, amused tolerance with which adults respond to children who are doing their best to act grown up.

"Menus," he said. Then, as though trying to put a difficult idea simply, "Menus are all very well in their place. To be sure, they can confuse the irresolute and embarrass those who do not know the dishes or the language." A glint in her green-gray eyes led him to add hastily during the translation, "Neither of which, of course, applies to the *signora*.

"But we have no need of menus here," he went on smoothly. "I know food, the markets, and how my wife, a good woman, cooks. I choose the meal. It is very good. My patrons like it; see how happy these people are." And, indeed, they were happy, if not hilarious. "So," he ended, "enjoy yourselves, drink some wine, and, in a moment, you shall see."

The strife was over. Dionysus was in command and we had joined in the rites. They began almost at once. A large bottle of local wine, and very fair it was, was soon followed by another; then the hors d'oeuvres, largely unknown to me, except for the *prosciutto*, the paper-thin Italian ham wrapped around pieces of melon. After that came fish broiled over charcoal, skinned and filleted by Dionysus, and covered with lemon juice, herbs, and butter. After that, chicken broiled the same way, juicy and tender, served with beans and Italian bread with garlic butter.

By this time my companion seemed to be falling behind the rest of us. Dionysus, who had been clattering about serving and talking to everyone, was onto it in a moment, standing at her side, peering anxiously at her plate. "Delicious," she murmured, "but you are too generous."

"Ah, no, *Signora,* it is not good for ladies to watch their figures. Nature intended that others should do this." A satyrish glance indicated that this was by no means an unpleasurable occupation, and brought a slight blush.

"To look like this (sucking in his cheeks) is not good for ladies, and makes them unkind to gentlemen. When the cheeks are full (blowing them out), ladies smile more and everything goes better. Think of my wife when I say, 'Your best did not tempt the *signora'.*"

So there was nothing for it but finish the chicken and the salad and the wine.

Things began to get complicated with dessert. A little table was put beside us and on it two bowls, one of sliced apples, the other of sliced pears. Over the apples Dionysus poured gin, over the pears, Cointreau. Innumerable lemons were squeezed over each, and lots of sugar. Finally apples and pears were well mixed. The result seemed food for gods—that is, gods who would like the island on a Sunday afternoon, not egg-head gods like Athene or Apollo. A great sense of well-being came over us as we waited for coffee and liqueurs.

They came in an unexpected way. By skilled conducting, Dionysus had brought all his patrons to the concluding point at the same time, regardless of when they had begun. All were ready for their coffee. The boy, a solemn acolyte, placed on a table in the center of the terrace a large bowl resting in a frame containing a spirit lamp which he lighted and trimmed. Dionysus appeared with a number of bottles and some packages of sugar. As conversation died, the acolyte scurried back and forth to the kitchen pouring pots of coffee into the bowl, and carefully arranging the bottles as for a rite. The quiet deepened as we all strained to catch the opening words.

"This is the time of year," Dionysus began, gently touching his bottles, "for the harvest festival, as it was over two and a half thousand years ago in my Sicily, in those beautiful Greek temples we still have, built when Rome was a village and before there was even the little Etruscan temple to Demeter on the Aventine. Then it was that the rites were held to Demeter, the mother of all, to Ceres, who brought life and growth, and to him who had in special charge the vine which drives away the cares of man and smooths his brow, Dionysus." I would have sworn that at the last word he gave the merest suggestion of a bow.

"The rites began," he went on, "with the bowl placed on the altar and filled, as it has been here." From a table off to one side came, *sotto voce,* "I didn't know that the Greeks had coffee."

"Ah, my friend, there is much that one does not know about the Greeks. One does not know, for instance, that they did *not* have coffee. But it matters little what liquid filled the bowl. Importance lay in

62

what was added. To Demeter, greatest of all, the distillation of the grape." The boy handed him a bottle of brandy, and in it went. "To Ceres, who cherished and nourished her children, the soothing and gentle white wine." In went a bottle of Suave. "And to him who gives strength for gaiety and laughter and dancing when the day's work is done, the foaming red wine." A bottle of Chianti. "For the god of each village and each field, the flavoring which they have given." Cinnamon, cloves, and grated nutmeg. "Finally to honor all those, young and old, men and women, whose backs have bent and whose hands have gathered, innumerable as the grains of this sugar, I add it also."

"But, you are no *agricoltore*," a voice came from behind me. "What do you harvest?"

He exploded with a burst of triumphant laughter. "My friend, my dear friend, I began to fear that I must talk all afternoon before one of you would help me by asking that. My harvest? My harvest will be the lira, the beautiful lira, you will soon pay me. Is not that the most precious harvest? To be sure, the rest of the world does not think much of our lira. But we Italians are true to it, so true that the less it is worth the more we want."

"Isn't it the truth?" someone remarked amid the laughter, clapping, and bravos. The sacrificial coffee was served. The sun was dropping toward the hills. There was a general scraping of chairs. We moved toward the steps where the harvest was being stored in another bowl, a sort of classical cash register, to the accompaniment of farewells and much joking. As my change was being retrieved from the bowl, I said quietly, *"Addio, Dionysus dell'isola."* He looked up quickly. "The *signore* spoke?"

"Only to say thank you and good-by."

"Mille grazie," he beamed. *"Ma non addio, arrivederci ad un'altra volta."* Not good-by, so long, until another time.

The Errant Vaporetto

Venice had put on her best September frock, deep blue splashed with gold and stirred by a breeze from the Adriatic. We were to meet by the boat landing in front of the Accadèmia at eleven-thirty, leaving plenty of time to cross the island for the twelve-fifteen vaporetto to Burano for lunch. Half the pleasure of these carefully arranged and timed meetings was to get there first and watch the arrival of the other two with their differing agitations. So I arrived early and established myself at a table in the shade with a *caffè esprèsso*.

Our host could be counted on to arrive on the dot. He would at once start to consult his watch and peer anxiously at each group of disembarking passengers and every pedestrian in the little square. My companion would be late, the constant victim of perverse event—the laggard watch, the unexpected friend, the

The Reporter, September 15, 1960.

gondola ferry caught in violent altercation across the Canal. Today this was almost a sure thing, as she was going first to a show of contemporary painting, then to the Accadèmia for the restorative effect of its Tintorettos and Veroneses. The meeting was certain to be in the classic style.

But it was not at all. As the half hour struck from a dozen churches, our host stepped from a boat to the landing, and my companion came out of the gallery putting away her glasses, wholly unperturbed. This expedition, I thought, is beginning with an ominous smoothness.

The sense of dangerously smiling fortune came again as we landed at the Rialto after a short run up the Canal. Usually a party must expect to be separated and perhaps, to have one of its members carried on to the next stop in the spirited scrimmage between landing and boarding passengers. This is, of necessity, short and sharp, since the stop is a mere pause beside the landing, with no nonsense about tying up or gangways. The movements off and on take place simultaneously over a sporting hazard of open water, and seem to support the observation that God is on the side of the big battalions. This time we had power behind us. With our female figurehead in the prow we cut through the weaker incoming tide and reached the landing intact, if breathless.

Fortune smiled, too, on the overland journey from the Canal to the vaporetto's berth on the water front facing the great lagoon made by the barrier reef. Here we plunged into a labyrinth—narrow, twisting, and forked lanes, lined with shops and filled from wall to wall with eddying humanity. It was too much to hope not to lose a man now and then in the maze. One hoped rather not to lose so many so often that, finally, the boat at the end of the journey was lost too. Human currents swirling up and down the lanes, in and out of shops, crosscurrents striking them from converging alleys, pushcarts cutting through the crowds, jams at bridges over innumerable small canals—all this made any formation but single file impossible and could cut off sheep from the bellwether in that scriptural minimum of time, the twinkling of an eye. There, at one moment almost at arm's length, would be the back one was following; in the next it was gone, perhaps whirled away by an enfilading tide, perhaps vanished around a corner while one was caught in a nightmarish block.

But this time only the last man was lost, and he only twice. Early training in the north woods had taught him when lost to stay still and wait to be found. To run around was fatal. The rule proved as sound in Venice as in Maine. So we reached the vaporetto with fifteen minutes to spare, and thereby nearly met disaster.

At the end of the pier two small steamers were tied up, one outboard of the other. After getting our tickets, we strolled casually aboard the nearer and followed my companion, who pointed to empty seats in the stern. There we watched the busy comings and goings of a water front until a bell, a whistle, and throbbing announced impending action—but not on our vaporetto. It was a close thing, but we made it after the ship had begun to move, and to the cheers of both ships' companies.

"Do you know," I asked when I had breath enough to speak, "about the Judas goats in the stockyards who lead the foolish, trusting sheep to destruction?"

"Speaking of goats," she said, "as I remember it, you two found the ship. I found the seats; and they were good seats."

"Perhaps now," our host interposed gently, "you might find some more. It doesn't look easy." This, I thought, is what comes of a good start, the most dangerous of beginnings.

Separated and wedged in among our fellow voyagers, we were not, as the saying goes, left alone with our thoughts. Within the limits of linguistic capability, we shared theirs. This did not involve eavesdropping. As their talk broke over me like surf, sometimes giving me a good roll and filling my ears with sound, I began to speculate on the capacity of various peoples to express high spirits in decibels. The first generalization—that it came with Latin blood—had to be discarded when I thought of the carrying power of the Negro church social in our Maryland village. Then social status—the idea that to be noisy was "vulgar" —had to go when one remembered the cocktail parties that had deafened one, or, mercifully, turned one back by their ample warning of the horror ahead.

But the cocktail party gave the clue. It was absence

of inhibition. Healthy people having a good time are naturally noisy. They compete for attention. They give out loud laughs and happy shouts. All children act this way; and adults, in the degree that innate vitality, alcohol, or lack of repressive training, or a combination of all three, loosens the inhibitions which society imposes by that most ubiquitous of all secret police, self-consciousness. Italians need less alcohol than most. Bubbling with vitality, they have never believed that silence was golden, or that the murmured understatements of the high tables at Oxford or Cambridge represented fun at its gayest.

So the vaporetto throbbed with sound above as well as below deck. Sound and odor seemed to envelop us in a little mist of our own, the odor of oil and diesel fumes from the engine room, the odor of drains from the lagoon, the odor of a dozen varieties of salami being unwrapped around us. Happy, noisy, and fragrant, we throbbed our way past the island cemetery, past Murano with its factories, and along the line of channel buoys, each with its seagull sentinel.

For me, seated aft in the vaporetto facing the stern, the scene brought back another life and world, the world of the lowly jump seat in my grandmother's victoria from which I gazed up at the lofty figures of my mother and grandmother made even more towering by parasols. The only way to look out was sideways and back, a sure invitation to the embarrassing carriage malady; better to look upward and inward and to concentrate on the often baffling talk.

Stories

So it was on the vaporetto, until craning necks near the rail brought hope of a landfall, like the branches seen by Columbus on the water. Bells jangled below. Engines stopped. The vaporetto lost way. But nothing happened, none of the preparations for a landing. We simply drifted, a practice regarded contemptuously in the modern world, but one ideally suited to the vaporetto's navigational problem, as was soon revealed to us backward-lookers. She was attempting, it appeared, to pass a dredge and its attendant barges in a narrow channel where the dredge was working. To drift onto the mud flat would do little harm, since a quick reverse of the propeller could remedy that. But to be pushed on under power was another matter. Tugs or tide, or both, might need hours to free us.

Though our movement was almost imperceptible, the talk between dredge and vaporetto was fast and spirited enough. To the two crews it was obviously a resumption of jovial vocational insult. But the note of badinage between dredge and passengers was spicy, if not downright ribald, punctuated by bursts of laughter and protests of *"Che orrore!"* from female passengers singled out for comment.

Once past the dredge, we soon reached Burano for luncheon, an almost biological experience, introduced by a tour of the kitchen to make our choices among denizens of the surrounding waters, more plausible as specimens in a laboratory than as luncheon dishes. But they presented an array of novel and surprisingly pleasant tastes and textures, helped on their way by a potable local white wine. All of this took its own good time and then called for rest on the shady side of the village square, so that after a leisurely stroll around Torcello and its eleventh-century church—with the only stone shutters I have ever seen—we just made the landing for the vaporetto's last homeward trip of the afternoon. As she came in, it looked as though all Venice had had the same idea and that not one ample body of the goodly company waiting could be squeezed aboard. But a miracle was accomplished. No one was left behind. No one was crowded overboard. The propeller churned a muddy whirlpool and off we moved.

Pushed by the crowd behind, I squeezed through those ahead and once more found a place in the stern, hopelessly separated from my friends. So close was the wooden seat to the one facing it that achievement of a decorous adjustment of knees and feet with the stout lady across from me would have been difficult had not her companion been a very little girl. So little that her legs stuck straight out in front of her, and she still had long curls, the starched short dress that makes little girls look like ballet dancers and professional skaters, and a straw hat with long ribbons behind and elastic under her chin. The time had not yet come for her—about four, perhaps—when the delicate elfin, often breathtaking quality of the small female child goes into its long eclipse, a time of pigtails and straight hair and bands on the teeth, a time of being too skinny or too fat, too noisy or too shy.

Stories

Into this ungainly and unlikely chrysalis she disappears for a decade or so, to emerge, as Alfred Noyes's singing seaman reported of the phoenix, "with wings of gold and emerald, most beautiful to see."

Hoping to appease the stout lady for crowding her, I murmured with a benign glance at the little girl, *"Com' è carina!"* But the stout lady had evidently had a hard day. With no attempt at benignity, she shot back something to the effect that "pretty is as pretty does," and added that looks did not make a *serafina.* This depressed the little girl as well as me. We thought it unwise even to smile at one another.

Happily, the constraint was broken by the stopping of the engines with the slight anxiety which that always causes when unexpected. In our immediate vicinity I alone knew what was up; but I could not think of the Italian word for a dredge. It was just too simple—*"una draga."* My attempt to get around the block by *"un vapore cavare della terra"*—a steamship to dig up the ground—deepened the mystery. But only for a moment. As the presence of the dredge ahead was learned from those by the rail, my contribution was revealed as that of a master humorist. Even the stout lady was restored to good humor and the little girl, after patient explanation had been made, fell victim to uncontrollable giggles. *"A vapore* to dig up the ground"—what a wag!

As we drifted abreast the dredge, the salty exchange of the morning was repeated. One of our company in the stern soon established herself as the leader of repartee on the vaporetto. Appropriately, she stood.

The Errant Vaporetto

In front of the crescent-shaped row of seats along the stern rail was an open space for standees, interspersed with stanchions for them to hold onto. She was holding one of these with one hand while the other gestured her sallies, cocking a snook or shaking a gay fist at her opponents. Her clothes, the worn black skirt and jacket, the handkerchief over her head, proclaimed her a working woman, but her mobile face, the dancing mischief in her eyes, and the slightly cracked voice which made what she said funny even before she finished saying it, proclaimed her a character. No blushes or *"che orrores"* for her. She gave as good as she got, the saltier the better. One could see her in the Place de la Revolution, the Vengeance incarnate, not counting and knitting like Mme. Defarge, but shouting her cruel jokes as the unfortunate aristocrats "sneezed into the basket." As the little girl exuded charm and the stout lady respectability, so Mme. Stanchion exuded vitality.

At length, as in the morning, the period of drift ended as bells sounded below; this time, so it seemed, more insistently. The engine gave a great shudder. The propeller shot us ahead. With a resounding crash, the vaporetto hit an immovable object and stopped dead.

The ensuing demonstration in physics was unforgettable. Instantly the momentum of the ship was transferred to all unattached objects capable of forward movement—most poignantly for me, to the little girl and her mother. The former shot off her seat and under mine, where she set up a commendable contribution to the developing pandemonium. The stout lady, with a higher trajectory and muzzle velocity, completely blanketed what a recent book has referred to as "target you." Only the merciful resilience of her prow prevented the camera hung around my neck from merging into a lung.

All around us our fellow passengers presented varying versions of the Laocoön statue, entangled as they were with one another. Shouts, shrieks, laughter, and profanity impeded the effort to persuade the unwilling aggressors in these embraces—the stout lady, for one—that no immediate disaster impended and that their indicated course was moderate speed astern. At length it was accomplished. The stout lady returned to her seat. The little girl was retrieved from under mine in good order, though still apprehensive.

Apparently, the vaporetto had achieved a most unusual maneuver. When almost past the dredge complex, in a narrow channel, with no way on at all, it had responded to the call for engines by ramming something solid with very respectable force. Time, and a good deal of declamation and denunciation, established no damage to dredge or vaporetto and no apparent casualties. As we got under way at last, my watch told me that we should be late for our tea engagement. Our host, a ready worrier, sought me out to urge us to meet at the gangway to be early off the boat and on our way.

Meanwhile a new drama was unfolding nearby.

The Errant Vaporetto

The lady of the stanchion had once more become the center of attention. Articulate and dramatic, she held her audience as she demonstrated some anguishing malady of the neck, right shoulder, and arm. Interest grew. Sympathy appeared to be turning into partisanship.

I pressed the stout lady into service. Relieved now of anxiety, our late intimacy had established a definite camaraderie. She listened and explained. The lady of the stanchion had been painfully injured. Thrown against the stanchion, a great stiffness was overcoming her whole right side, as one could plainly see. *"Che peccato!"* How could the poor woman scrub the floors on which her living depended? What would become of her children (of whom none seemed to be in evidence)? Justice must be done, announced the stout lady. What were courts and lawyers for, anyway? For a moment panic seized me, as I thought that by some intuition she knew my secret. I saw myself acquiring the ideal client not to have. But the question was purely rhetorical. Obviously, courts and lawyers were good for nothing, as any sensible person knew.

At this point a little man in a dirty white coat and nautical cap bustled up, began questioning the lady of the stanchion and taking notes on the back of an envelope. She, who a moment before had been animation itself, relapsed at once into a languor undoubtedly induced by pain. But her feeble replies were readily supplemented by the surrounding company. Volubly and with considerable, though not always consistent, virtuosity, they described the catastrophe following the horrendous crash. Whitecoat's irritation grew with his bewilderment and the confusion of his notes. He held up his hands imploring quiet, stared fixedly at the envelope, and asked, "The left side, was it?"

As one man, the whole company in the stern let out an indignant roar: "The right side, you fool, the right side! Can't you see?"

The poor man was metaphorically blown back to the deckhouse. As he scuttled away, the drooping victim blazed into action. Shaking her right fist high above her head, she hurled an imprecation at this unhappy proletarian slave of a state monopoly. "Capitalistic pig!" she screamed.

The defeat of the common enemy unified the company under the warrior queen. Her spirits, wit, and verve took us the rest of the way to Venice. We separated as a general movement began toward the gangway.

I was hurrying along the wharf to join my friends when the sight of an ambulance off to one side was not to be resisted. Beside it was a small crowd, in the center of which were the lady of the stanchion, whitecoat, and a young intern, who was moving her right arm slowly up and down, like one examining a pump handle for the first time. Forlorn and outnumbered, her fiery spirit seemed quenched under the weight of professional skepticism. As I turned away, there, the embodiment of indignation, stood the stout lady, who had been watching too. It was plain to see that she had caught the torch as it fell from the limp hand by the ambulance. To the surprise and delight of the little girl, the stout lady fired her broadside. A little quaveringly, a little primly, but firmly enough, she shouted, "Capitalistic pigs!"

Mme. Stanchion looked up, straightened up, and smiled. The little girl smiled; the stout lady smiled; I smiled.

"*Arrivederci!*" we said.

Part Three ⫷⫷⫷

*History, Law, and
Lawyers*

History as Literature

The practice of your society in discussing each year the subject "History as Literature" is reminiscent of the Oxford Club, which tested prospective members by presenting each with a saucer containing three cooked prunes and a spoon, and asking each to eat the prunes. The problem, of course, seemed to be what to do with the pits. Should they be delicately extruded into the spoon and returned to the saucer? Or into a cupped hand, to the same destination? Or dropped there directly? Swallowing them would seem to dodge, not meet, the test. Perhaps, however, the disposition of the prune pits was not the true test. Perhaps it was how the victim dealt with a situation having little or no meaning in itself. Here could be an experiment of considerable

Address given before the Society of American Historians, Washington, D.C., March 31, 1966, and published in *Esquire,* October, 1966.

natural interest to historians.

In his inaugural lecture as Regius Professor of History at Cambridge in 1895, Lord Acton touched on the relation between history and literature.

" 'Politics,' said Sir John Seeley, 'are vulgar when they are not liberalised by history, and history fades into mere literature when it loses sight of its relation to practical politics.' "

"Everybody," continued Lord Acton, "perceives the sense in which this is true. For the science of politics is the one science that is deposited by the stream of history, like grains of gold in the sand of a river; and the knowledge of the past, the record of truths revealed by experience, is eminently practical, as an instrument of action, and a power that goes to the making of the future. . . ."

These two scholars took a dim view, a contemptuous view of history as literature, "mere literature," and they came to it because of their conception of the nature of history. To Sir John Seeley history should be a liberalizer of politics, performing (apparently) somewhat the same function as modern products advertised as tenderizers of meat. Lord Acton in one sentence sees history as a stream and also as a "power that goes to the making of the future." We catch the note of determinism, echoed in almost the same metaphor in the preface to Sir Steven Runciman's account of *The Fall of Constantinople, 1453*. He writes, "Nowadays we know too well that the stream of history flows on relentlessly and there is never a barrier across it." To some, in this nuclear age, it is not so clear that even life, surely the raw material of history, must flow on without some pretty good management not obviously foreordained.

However, to Lord Acton both the relentless flow and its direction were clear. More and more it came to him as a Hegelian conception, the unfolding of an idea; and the idea was that of liberty.

Karl Marx, grubbing in the British Museum, preparing the time bomb which was to go off with shattering effect long after his death, had the same Hegelian conception, but a different idea. His idea was primarily economic, dialectical materialism. Others have seen other ideas relentlessly unfolding. I mention the determinist theory of history with diffidence to a group which knows far more about it than I only to suggest that it offers rocky soil for history as literature. Those to whom the end and the path to it must be taken as known must write about the past in a way designed to comfort the faithful or convert or confound the heathen. This is not likely to produce literature. Parts of the Bible may be offered in evidence against me, but little modern narrative. For the most part purposeful writing is apt to be dull. I can produce volumes of bound briefs to prove it. To be sure, at times Soviet historical writing is amusing, but only because it reads like a parody of *The Secret Life of Walter Mitty*.

Some other theories of history, also, lead to stunted literature, among them history as teacher, judge, or jury. The phrase, "history teaches us that," usually precedes bald statement of the writer's principal thesis, often incapable of other support. It reminds us of the marginal note of the preacher in his sermon, "Weak point, shout!"

For history as judge, we go back to Lord Acton's lecture.

". . . I exhort you never to debase the moral currency or to lower the standard of rectitude, but to try others by the final maxim that governs your own lives, and to suffer no man and no cause to escape the undying penalty which history has the power to inflict on wrong. . . .

"History does teach," thundered his Lordship, citing Froude in support, "that right and wrong are real distinctions," and "the moral law is written on the tablets of eternity."

In short, history, as the teaching judge, is not the stern daughter of the voice of God, but the very voice of God itself, and of a God whose judgments are unadulterated by mercy. If the writings of prophets explaining these judgments are literature, and sometimes they are, it will not be the literature of the Psalms or of Ecclesiastes but of Elijah pronouncing judgment on the priests of Baal or of Lincoln in the Second Inaugural interpreting the Civil War:

"Yet if God wills that it [this mighty scourge of war] continue until all the wealth piled by the bondsman's two hundred and fifty years of unrequited toil shall be sunk, and until every drop of blood drawn with the lash shall be paid by another drawn with the sword, as was said three thousand years ago, so still it must be said, 'The judgments of the Lord are true and righteous altogether.' "

Two years earlier Charles Francis Adams had confided to his diary the same thought. "Perhaps it is part of the Divine dispensation that the hearts of these people remain hardened until the end of emancipation be accomplished."

These views produce solemn, if sonorous, literature, and—if a layman may venture an opinion—dangerous history. Was it, perhaps, this view of things which led Lord Macaulay to write both? It helps one to find truth in one's prejudices, which are pre-judgments— that is, made before considering all available evidence. God is the most powerful of all allies. The late Congressman Sol Bloom was fond of quoting his mother's saying, "One with God is a majority." The majority does not need the support of evidence. For is not it, too, the voice of God? *Vox populi, vox dei.* It is the same, whether the judgment is one of condemnation or vindication. Some recent writers might have done well to recall a wise observation: "Praise is the shipwreck of historians; his preferences betray him more than his aversions."

When we move from the conception of history as judge to history as jury, a new and realistic idea enters the field. Czar Reed, the Speaker of the House of Representatives, writes Barbara Tuchman, declared "that 'the verdict of history' was the only one worth recording and he was confident of its outcome." Now a verdict is the product of a jury, under the Anglo-American legal system, its unanimous opinion, and its opinion upon the facts. The law is given to the jury by the judge; but both come out in the verdict as a rather scrambled egg. This is particularly true in cases arousing strong emotions, as, for instance, those involving extracurricular sexual relations. Here the jury may apply its own unwritten law, usually that any woman may shoot, stab, but not poison, any man; less often, that the wronged male may similarly liquidate either or both offending members of the triangle.

"Les Anglo-Saxons," as General de Gaulle refers to the practitioners of the jury system, regard it as an excellent method of administering law tempered by justice. But its most ardent admirer would hardly advocate it as an adequate way of establishing truth, at least as truth is conceived by a physical scientist.

The conception of history as a verdict does, however, make a contribution, in fact, two contributions. In the first place, we do not look to verdicts for literature. They are as sparing of words as Calvin Coolidge. A verdict may be "guilty," "not guilty," "guilty with a recommendation for mercy," "verdict for the plaintiff" or defendant; perhaps most useful for historical purposes, the Scotch verdict, "not proven." In short, the verdict gives us only ultimate conclusions; not even a "special verdict" explains. This is not such stuff as literature is made on. The other contribution is that a verdict is the collective conclusion of a group. In other words, what we are talking about is the verdict of *historians*.

What "comfortable words," as the Book of Common Prayer puts it, these are! They reassure us that Man is not a poor creature caught in the jaws of fate. They let us out of the courtroom, the school-room, and rescue us from the relentless stream. When Mr. Lincoln said that "we cannot escape history"— "we, even we here"—he meant that we cannot escape historians, escape from being written about, gossiped about, and, perhaps, made the target of epithets. This is a tolerable fate. "Sticks and stones will break my bones," says the nursery rhyme, "but names will never hurt me." The aphorism may not be wholly true, but it is good advice to work from and frees us to go on to follow that of Mark Twain: "Always do right. This will gratify some people and astonish the rest." It restores free will, for man is on his own to decide in that instant between past and future.

While public men cannot escape historians, they would do well to forget about them while they get on with their job. One cannot even be sure of fixing the jury by employing its members—though it may help temporarily—or by becoming a member and writing its verdict, as Sir Winston Churchill said that he would do.

If I may be diverted by my King Charles's head, I would suggest that to have a sense of history, in the current phrase, may be a dangerous weakness in a public man. The phrase seems to suggest finding the test of action in the approval of a fancied future, rather than a present majority; or, put differently, in imagining oneself appearing well in a great pageant of human life, reaching back into the mists and moving on into the clouds. In any event, it is a form of concern with one's self or, in the vulgarized synonym, one's image. The great corrupter of public men is the ego—corrupter because distracter. Wealth, sensuality, power cannot hold a candle to it. Looking into the mirror distracts one's attention from the problem. The solution of every problem, every achievement is, as Justice Holmes said, a bird on the wing; and, he added, one must have one's whole will focused in one's eye on that bird. One cannot be thinking of one's self or one's image or one's place in history— only of that bird. Regarding the much praised sense of history, I would say to you historians, borrowing from a cartoon in *The New Yorker:* "Gentlemen of the jury, it's spinach and to hell with it!"

Returning to my theme, the conclusion that history is the product of historians makes a vast contribution to a discussion of history as literature, for the product of historians is writing and writing is the beginning of literature. Mrs. Tuchman complains that Richard Strauss attempted with his music "a non-musical function: making it describe characters, emotions, events and philosophies, which is essentially the function of literature." It is essentially the function of historians, too, taking the word "philosophies" to mean investigations of what underlies human nature and conduct—sometimes horrendously called behavioral science. If history is thought of as a tale, the story of man's multifarious adventures on this earth, what led him, moved him, or left him passive for long, dark centuries, the arts of literature must give it life—literature in no narrow sense, not merely well-parsed prose, not merely good writing. The first lady of Parnassus, Calliope, the Muse of Epic Poetry, inspired Homer, Virgil, the composers of the sagas, and perhaps a little that otherwise dour Scot, Thomas Carlyle. What differentiates history from *Who's Who* or the encyclopedia is the art with which literature transforms mere compilation of research.

This art must be one sternly disciplined to its purpose, to give life to a story strictly measured and controlled by fact. The historian, like Pygmalion, must watch out not to pray for too much life or his loved work may turn into "My Fair Lady." Some years ago a colleague in the State Department wrote papers in such beautiful prose that I found myself influenced toward conclusions which, when challenged, I could not justify. Protection against this siren proved fairly simple. Another colleague rewrote the paper in telegraphese, leaving out all articles, most adjectives, and unessential verbs, inserting the word "stop" for periods, and after the negative "not," adding "repeat not." This exorcised the magic. Too much art in the mixture and, in Sir John Seeley's contemptuous words, "history fades into mere literature."

If history is a story, it is a story about people. Prehistory can be a story, too, and great literature, as Jacquetta Hawkes in *The Land* and Loren Eiseley in *The Immense Journey* have amply shown. A story about people requires a theme, a theme about specific doings at a specific time and place, about what caused them and where they led. The theme is improved by limitations. Brave men have attempted the History of Mankind, but one may doubt whether they brought it off, and, even more, that the result was literature. To attempt to tell all about everything can result in telling very little about anything. In history, as elsewhere, modesty is a virtue. It may be even more a necessity, with the vast expansion of our knowledge about the nature and complexity of the human mind and emotions as well as the record of the past.

"In this story" (of the fall of Constantinople), writes Sir Steven Runciman, "the Greek people is the tragic hero." *"Arma virumque cano,"* sang Virgil. A hero of a sort or, at least, a central figure or group is nearly essential to any story. Today, it is true, some things called "forces"—economic forces, psychological forces, and so on—enter historical analysis and, like smog, poison the air necessary for literature. Consider this sentence "by a Pulitzer prize-winning historian," as the jacket blurb calls him: "The process by which Congress came to pass this legislation can best be described in quasi-mechanical terms as an equilibrium achieved by a resolution of quantitatively measurable forces." I agree wholly with Mr. David Donald's conclusions in his *The Politics of Reconstruction, 1863–1867.* I even agree that his language helps prove his novel points to doubting professional colleagues. If some things, as has been said, must be stated obscurely before they can be stated clearly, the third step may hopefully be to state them with artistry.

What Mr. Donald is writing about is not so abstruse or forbidding as "an equilibrium achieved by a resolution of quantitatively measurable forces"; he is writing about people. His point is that, if a community is divided into groups with mutually irreconcilable purposes, it may be impossible to construct a consensus powerful enough to control and operate the very complicated government set up by our Constitution to deal with an excruciatingly difficult problem. The problem under discussion was the incorporation of four million black people in the South into the American democracy.

If after Appomattox Southerners had come back into the community as members in good standing, the Democrats would almost certainly have regained their former position as the permanent national majority. Lincoln's plan to prevent this was to split the Democrats by concessions and attach enough to his party to keep control. Accordingly, he looked for support in Congress to the war Democrats and the city Republicans who themselves needed Democratic votes to be returned. The rural Republicans, for the most part with safe seats and increasing with the population and popular feeling, would take no such chance. For them the rebels would have no more part in running things. The South would remain occupied and under military control, until the loyalists, selected freedmen, and reconstructed Southerners could be relied upon to do the right thing—in any event, for a long time. They would have approved of war trials, a denazification program, and economic and social reforms carried out by competent occupation administrations like those of General Clay in Germany and General MacArthur in Japan. The Radicals' desires suffered from two impediments. They did not have the majority to carry them out; and they did not realize the ephemeral power of an occupation. The result is what we know. The race problem remained as recalcitrant, perhaps more so because larger and more widespread, for President Johnson in 1965 as for President Johnson in 1865.

The new interpretation should improve, not harm, the literature of the Reconstruction period. Hitherto, the Reconstruction period has been depicted with sentimentality and bathos, a story made for filming by Cecil B. De Mille. Mr. Donald opens a day for new and better books.

In the development of history as literature first comes the choice of theme for the story, the author's choice of the tale he will tell and his interpretation of all the facts he can find which bear on it. Notice I have said "all the facts," not all the truth. Facts, as often as not, are ambiguous. They are not all created free and equal. They must all be fairly considered, though not in telling the story, and hopefully the author's interpretation of the facts will be his idea of truth. For instance, I am prepared to accept the fact that Henry II in thorough exasperation cried out, "Who will free me from this turbulent priest?" It is not, however, established truth that he wished certain courtiers to respond by murdering the Archbishop. The same may, perhaps, be said about the remark of President Kennedy's referring to one of his senior cabinet colleagues. However, the same incitement to elminination has been attributed to it. Are we sure that when Pilate asked, "What is truth?" he was really jesting? Or that, if he had stayed, he would have received a helpful answer?

While being true to fact, we need not be such purists as to shrink from a little imagination to garnish it. Thucydides used it with adequate warning. We may rely, he tells us, on his account of the Peloponnesian War as coming from eyewitnesses, himself and others. But the speeches in the story, he admits, are his own. In those happy days, before the duplicator and recorder, words were ephemeral. He writes what the speakers would and should have said if they were true to their own positions and to the occasions. Who is in a position to complain? Certainly not Pericles, whose funeral oration has become immortal; nor we who read it. We might even gain if today you historians wrote speeches for the great, instead of the anonymous scribes who do—with two exceptions; I would not substitute you for Lincoln or Churchill.

With the theme settled, comes the manner of its telling. The first requirement is to catch and hold the reader. Justice Holmes's uncle, Charles Jackson, got to the heart of the matter when he said, "Wendell, if you forget the color of the heroine's eyes, drop that book!" He has supported me in the comforting belief that after seventy I no longer need to read a book which bores me, regardless of what the critics say.

There are many ways to tell a tale and hold a reader, but to begin with, the writer must carry conviction that he has a tale to tell, that he believes it, is full of it, and wants to get on with it. The wise writer chooses a subject adapted to his style, which is himself. Carlyle writes of the French Revolution with fire caught from the holocaust itself. Though his work is thought less of today than it was decades ago when some of us read him, he left unforgettable pictures on the mind. Episodes took on symbolic meaning. The flight to Varennes epitomized the stolid, stupid, yet sometimes gallant, futility of the *ancien régime*—the lumbering monarch and the lumbering berlin, the silly plan foolishly executed, the pretty, flighty queen slowing the already glacial pace, the faithful Count Fersen, himself destined to die at the hands of another mob in another revolution. Told by a master storyteller, the suspense of impending doom becomes unendurable. Carlyle's day passed with the Romantic Movement. We know now that there is more to history than the story of great men, though a wise man would not have said so too confidently in the presence of Sir Winston Churchill. Nevertheless, when all is said, Carlyle's history must still retain a high rating as literature.

This Wagnerian style would not do at all for the theme chosen by Lord David Cecil in his biography of Lord Melbourne. Here was needed a more muted mode, a more sensitive understanding of more delicate situations, less flamboyant emotions, a more private tragedy. The inducement of a literary Purcell or Debussy or Grieg was needed to lure back to life Lord Melbourne—the young Melbourne of the Age of Elegance with his own elegance and grace, his gifts, considerable when they could push through laziness, the long tragedy of his marriage to Lady Caroline Lamb;

94

then the middle-aged Melbourne conducting his mild autumn romance with the young queen while the dew was still on her and before the years of the matriarch surrounded by her innumerable progeny, of whom Lady Longford has given us such a surfeit. To me most understanding and touching of all is Lord David's description of the final years of loneliness. With the sustaining glamour of power and position withdrawn, his letters to the queen, the habit and joy of years, unanswered, friends dead or circling around another sun, with dimming faculties, he wanders through a silent house peopled by shadows.

The great advantage of biography as literature is that birth and death give it a beginning and an end. A few moments ago I suggested that, in choosing a historical theme—and I would now add in dealing with it —much is to be said for modesty. This is not to warn the historian against biting off more than he can chew, or indeed against its converse, chewing more than he has bitten off. It is to warn him against two other dangers. One is the limited quality of human persistence. We are told that the majority of all the people who have lived are now alive. I wonder how many of them have read all the way through Gibbon or Green or Lecky or Prescott or Parkman or many others who have produced monumental works. Of course, the question is a trick one and the answer proves nothing. But it suggests something about history as literature. It must be something that one can read. Even the Romans, using their Draconian methods, knew that there must be a limit to even the best banquet.

History, Law, and Lawyers

The other danger, particularly to writers of contemporary history and memoirs, is that these can so easily turn into collections of source material, strung together by narrative. This is not literature. Not all Sir Winston Churchill's gifts, apparent when he writes of his ancestors and his early life, save him from the trap of reprinting documents cemented by purple passages.

The historian has at hand literature's time-honored aids to understanding of character and scene. As old as Plutarch is the "little fact," the detail which reveals more of personality and event than the complex account of great moments. Consider this little fact about Lord Salisbury, Britain's Prime Minister at the turn of the century (again I am indebted to Mrs. Tuchman):

"His aloofness was enhanced by shortsightedness so intense that he once failed to recognize a member of his own Cabinet, and once, his own butler. At the close of the Boer War he picked up a signed photograph of King Edward and, gazing at it pensively, remarked, 'Poor Buller [referring to the Commander in Chief at the start of the war], what a mess he made of it.'"

If you look for insight into the kind of man General Marshall was, ponder another little fact, told to me by the General himself. During the Second World War a weekly news magazine published a pocket edition which the War Department distributed to the troops. One issue contained an article open to criticism as a grossly unfair attack on the President. An intimate of his and a member of the White House staff called on General Marshall reporting the President's wish that this issue be withheld from circulation to the

Army. The General replied, "Certainly. The President is the Commander in Chief. Kindly ask him to send his order to me in writing. It will be obeyed at once; and he will receive simultaneously my resignation as Chief of Staff of the Army." The matter was never mentioned again by anyone.

Or would you see Secretary Cordell Hull in typical mood? It is told of him that, when he was a judge in Tennessee, a friend, meeting him on the courthouse steps, asked him the time of day. Pulling out his gargantuan watch, the judge held it out. "You say first," he said.

Along with the little fact go other aids. Herbert Feis describes a meeting in the White House between President Hoover and President-elect Roosevelt and their advisers during the transition in 1933.

"Of the many confused scuffles it has been my professional pleasure to study, the one that ensued was the hardest to relate with confident accuracy. It was reminiscent of a naval engagement on a foggy night between two opposed fleets, each ship firing whenever a gun flash was seen, being quite as likely to blow up a friend as an enemy. In this instance as well, the proponents were shooting at shadows and hitting the air . . . each of the two groups suspected the other of secret purposes."

As time goes on, these aids to storytelling will remain and the story will remain one about people; but a theme will be harder to find, the fog of obscurity will grow. Not long ago a friend suggested that the day was not far off when in vast areas the name of Einstein would be more familiar than that of Churchill or Roosevelt, though many think him a Russian or a Chinese. More and more, modern science will affect the lives of people. Its achievements and equally its failures, as in the November blackout in the Northeast, may play a controlling part in the lives of millions. The historian may need the equivalent of an "inertial guidance system" to know his own position and the position of others. I have already suggested that some things must be stated obscurely before they can be stated clearly. Perhaps, too, new forms are needed to express what we yet see only through a glass darkly.

Something of this emerges from the reviews of Mrs. Tuchman's book, upon which I have drawn so heavily in this address. All agree upon the brilliance of her writing, recognize a verve, passion, and eloquence missing since Carlyle. But she puzzles her critics. Is *The Proud Tower* a jeremiad? Is its theme, as one reviewer would have it, "the contrast between the pomp and the privilege of the rich and the misery and desperation of the poor?" Another respected and thoughtful historian fears that her book suffers from the fatal defect of having no theme, no "thematic coherence," as he puts it. "If Mrs. Tuchman could have made explicit the subjective bases for her choices [of her various chapters] . . . given them shape and definition, she might thereby have raised them to the level of an organizing principle . . . we have instead not a 'portrait of the period,' but random brush strokes, leaving a canvas unoccupied by any ruling vision."

How often we have read the very words of this metaphor in criticisms of modern painting. Today in all the arts—verse, music, painting, sculpture—experimentation goes on to find new forms to express new interpretations of meaning and emotion. In response to all of them comes the complaint that the artist leaves too much to the reader, listener, or viewer. What does he mean? To some extent I share this view; but I recognize it as the result of my limitations, not those of the artists.

Mrs. Tuchman's portrait of a period is written in a different mode from G. M. Young's *Portrait of an Age,* which has all the beauty, clarity, and thematic coherence of a Reynolds. *The Proud Tower* conveys to me a period through which I lived. Reading the book I apprehend the people of the time and place as people possessed, as were the Gadarene swine and as lemmings often have been, by impulses which drove them to destruction. Her chapters give bearings on those impulses which are akin to madness or, to put it more mildly, obsession. The light she throws seems quite as helpful as the explanations of the Evangelists or the scientists. If none of them explain, I am content with the thought that beyond this conduct lies either nothing or, as a man wiser than I has said, "some vaster unthinkable to which every predicate is an impertinence."

The Prelude to Independence

The period from May 15 to July 4, 1776, has been happily called the prelude to independence. It could so easily—and so wrongly—have been called the prelude to revolution. But the truth about the American Revolution is that it was essentially what it claimed to be, the dissolution of the "political bands" which bound the colonies to the British crown and the assumption of a "separate and equal station" "among the powers of the earth." In other words, it was a political act, not a social revolution or a nationalist uprising, or a combination of the two, with which we are so familiar today.

The social and economic changes which, consciously or unconsciously, were being sought were not so great, I venture to say, conscious of my recklessness, as those

Address given at Williamsburg, Va., May 15, 1959. Published in *The Yale Review*, vol. XLVIII, No. 4 (June, 1959).

which led the American people in November 1932 to turn from the hope of salvation by faith to the doctrine of salvation by works.

As for nationalism, there was scarcely a trace of it. In fact, never was a nation so long and so reluctantly aborning. When it came, it seemed at the time more a mechanism than an organism. "Until well into the nineteenth century," Professor Boorstin tells us, "Jefferson—and he was not alone in this—was using the phrase 'my country' to refer to his native State of Virginia." Wholly absent, also, was the obverse of nationalism, xenophobia, that potent force which, in a flash, can whip up the mobs of Peiping, Cairo, or Bagdad. In fact, in the Declaration of Independence the eloquence of denigration was reserved solely for the villain of the piece, King George III, of unhappy memory. The British people are referred to as "our British [*sic*] brethren," and are gently chided because their "native justice and magnanimity" did not lead them to prevent the impairment of the hallowed rights of Englishmen.

A strange revolution, this, and one which should lead us to turn with keen interest to the two great documents of the prelude to independence—the Virginia Declaration of Rights and the Declaration of Independence. If we are struck with their similarity, we should not be surprised, since the authors of both were Virginians, members of a politically conscious class, and men widely read in English law—George Mason, in the library of his lawyer uncle, John Mercer of Marlborough; Jefferson, as a matter of professional training under the learned George Wythe. Both were superb legal draftsmen. We may note, too, that only one spokesman of a revolution of our own day was a lawyer—Lenin, who soon abandoned the practice to put his gloss on Marx. Stalin was trained for the priesthood; Hitler was a painter, Nasser and Kassem both colonels; and Mao Tse-tung got his training beyond normal school as an assistant in the library of the National Peking University, thus refuting Emerson's observation that "meek young men grow up in libraries." The modern revolutionary's view of lawyers has been more akin to that of Dick the Butcher in *Henry VI:* "The first thing we do, let's kill all the lawyers."

The construction of the two documents is basically the same. They both begin with a brief overture and move swiftly into the principal theme. Both overtures derive from the same concept; so do both themes. In each, the overture is spirited, emotional, romantic, a sparkling chain of generalities, the latest and most fashionable importation from France—the Rights of Man. Then, in each, follows the theme, sober, specific, practical, and English, the rights of Englishmen, the conception, not of an ethical or philosophical principle, but of a restraint on power itself. This carries the weight and significance of each document. Overture and theme are, of course, related, as all thought is related. Each has enriched the other. But they represent different approaches to a common problem and, even more important, different courses of experience.

The Rights of Man, with which each of our documents begins, are "self-evident" truths. "All men are created equal" and "endowed by their creator with certain inalienable Rights." Then follows the "social compact." Governments were instituted by equal and free men to secure these inalienable rights, derive their just powers from the consent of the governed, and may rightly be overthrown if they infringe upon inalienable rights. These truths had to be self-evident, for they rested upon no observed and recorded human experience. In the world of political thought they were the counterpart of Lafcadio Hearne's conception in romantic thought of the "eternal haunter," the vision of woman who has never existed. Both conceptions have inspired and bedeviled man.

Not long after the adoption of the Declaration of Rights at Williamsburg and of the Declaration of Independence at Philadelphia these abstract doctrines received more complete expression in the Declaration of the Rights of Man and the Citizen adopted on October 5, 1789, in the first stage of the French Revolution. Retained by the subsequent regimes of the First Republic, the Terror, and the Directory, the Rights of Man and the Citizen became the classic creed of European libertarians and eventually inspired similar statements throughout the world. A flurry of guarantees of natural rights accompanied the European revolts of 1830 and 1848, but most were short-lived. The winning of independence in South America brought other guarantees of rights, in this instance more directly influenced by the United States. Japan in the Constitution of 1889 adopted a declaration of rights and duties of the subject. The Czar followed in 1905; the Shah, in 1906; and the Sultan, in 1908. After the First World War came another flood—Germany, Austria, Poland, Afghanistan, Siam, and so on.

Today seventy-seven nations have in their basic law guarantees of natural rights. Included in the list are all the communist people's republics, except China. Their rights on paper are more extensive than ours. For instance, they guarantee the natural right to family, health, and motherhood, which does not appear in the basic law of the United States or the countries of the British Commonwealth, except India, which is losing enthusiasm for motherhood. Over fifty nations have accepted the Universal Declaration of Human Rights of the United Nations.

One would like to report that in fact the rights of the individual had become more secure and more respected as their verbal glorification has spread. But this is not the case. The great majority of these declarations of rights are, and remain, abstractions—one might almost say, in Lincoln's phrase, pernicious abstractions, for by pretending they deceive. To understand what gives reality to limitation upon power and security for individual rights we must turn to that other strand of human experience which is the more strongly stressed in our two documents.

The second and more important strand in the American documents was wholly different. The rights of Englishmen were not abstractions derived from speculation. They were the fruits of action, of strife. They were specific and detailed restraints upon power, to transgress which might—and on occasion did—mean death, and certainly meant a fight.

The very idea of a limitation upon power is a startling one. As Mr. Justice Holmes has said, "If you have no doubt of your premises or your power and want a certain result with all your heart you naturally express your wishes in law and sweep away all opposition." This is what the people's republics do. They have no doubt that their premises will achieve the happiness of man, or that their power is supreme; they desire their ends with all their hearts. So they enact revolutionary law, liquidate the counterrevolutionaries, and sweep aside the anti-party dissidents.

But Englishmen have put limitations upon the exercise of power itself. Where did this extraordinary idea come from and what in the soil of England made it grow uniquely there?

"In historical sequence," says a great scholar, "order precedes freedom." So it was in England. Immediately upon the conquest three Norman monarchs of great ability and insight, William I and Henry I and II, set about establishing a strong central government by profoundly modifying feudal institutions as they imported them from Normandy. The Conqueror, as McKechnie puts it, "encouraged the adoption in England of feudalism, considered as a system of land tenure and of social distinctions based on the possession of land; but he successfully checked the evils of its unrestrained growth as a system of local government and jurisdiction." The Norman kings rested their central authority on those foundations upon which any strong government must be based—a civil service of men of humble birth owing allegiance to the king; a local authority, the sheriff, also responsible to the king; a strong treasury which audited the sheriff's collections twice a year in London and by surprise visits in the counties. Nevertheless, as William and the two Henry's proceeded to build a strong monarchy, the feudal forces, which were to limit its power, were growing also.

All went well as long as the monarchy was successful. So long, that is, as taxes were bearable, administration was honest and capable, the king's justice remained a brand superior to that of the barons, and order was preserved. The barons grumbled over the king's growing power, but the country, and especially the towns, prospered. On the other hand, failure produced crisis. Richard's fecklessness and John's mismanagement drove the perfected financial machinery to squeeze ever higher taxation, and to impose new forms of it on merchandise and goods which hurt the towns. Ecclesiastical appointments were sold and so was justice. Three principal elements in the state were alienated from the monarchy—the barons, the Church, the freemen of the towns.

The result was revolt and Magna Carta. The Great Charter was a medieval and feudal document. In no sense was it revolutionary, forward-looking, or a declaration of the rights of man. The contemporary use of the word "Great" was not to describe its importance, but its length. The sixty-one clauses of the Charter were not statements of ideals, but of the law as it was. Here were definitions of relationships between the king and his vassals; solutions to specific points at issue between John and the barons; statements of procedures that the royal administration would henceforth follow; and extensions of certain limited rights to the Church, the towns, and the freemen, including, Congress will be interested to know, the right to leave and re-enter the kingdom "safe and secure by land and water."

Yet, in at least two respects the Charter contributed to the development of restraints on power in a broader fashion than the limited intentions of the barons might imply. First, it stated a medieval conception of kingship as contract between the overlord and his vassals, the validity of which depended upon performance. Here, in the principle that the ruler was restrained by law, was the kernel of constitutionalism. Second, in important instances the language of the Charter in forbidding specific violation by John of feudal law did so in language that later became the basis of far broader claims of right. The great example is the confirmation of judgment by peers provided by the Charter.

> No Freeman shall be taken, or imprisoned, or be disseised of his Freehold, or Liberties, or free Customs, or be outlawed, or exiled, or any otherwise destroyed; nor will we not pass upon him, nor condemn him, but by lawful Judgment of his Peers, or by the Law of the Land.

While this was by no means trial by jury, it was capable of being developed into that right with the evolution of legal procedure.

History, Law, and Lawyers

Two centuries and more of national experience with the practices and ideas of Magna Carta—the dispersal of domestic force among the landed proprietors, their control in Parliament of many forms of taxation, and specific and court-enforceable individual rights—had a profound effect when, later on, the national state was emerging. Its development was very different on either side of the channel. In France under the first Bourbons, guided at the outset by Cardinals Richelieu and Mazarin and brought to completion by Louis XIV, the barons were separated from their roots in the country by the bribe of privileges and wealth provided they became courtiers and dependents of the king. Very soon the control of all force in the kingdom was in the hands of the Sun King. His will was supreme because his power was.

The same forces at work in England produced two revolutions. While the Bourbons were making one national state, the Tudors and Stuarts were endeavoring to make another. The Tudors liquidated the last vestiges of the Middle Ages, ended the Wars of the Roses, and made a national state in England. But it was a society still carrying, not in its slogans, but in its law for which men fought, the specific, down-to-earth, procedural rights over which any arbitrary act stumbled and upon which the king's justices could be required to pass judgment.

This was a vast difference from what occurred across the channel. But it would not have endured but for another divergent course. In England the landed aristocracy did not surrender their power to the king and become courtiers living off his bounty. Quite the reverse. Under the Tudors, though their personnel changed, they increased their power by despoiling the Church. Elizabeth, imperious as she was, knew the limits of her power and the importance of inspiring a romantic attachment between herself and her people. Under Elizabeth, as under Victoria, the local force upon which the regime itself rested was controlled by the gentry who were the justices of the peace and local administrators. It did not rest upon a royal military establishment.

This irked the Stuarts, strongly influenced as they were from France and Spain. They pushed toward the concentration of domestic force and finance in the court. At one time under the able, vigorous leadership of Thomas Wentworth, Earl of Strafford, the chances seemed better than even that the tide of absolutism would engulf England as it was engulfing France. But Charles I did not have the stuff of dictatorship in him. The Civil War which was to destroy him broke out over his struggle to gain control over the ultimate instrument of coercion, armed force.

The curious fact is that for a brief span in the seventeenth century absolutism did triumph in England, but under Cromwell—or rather, under the New Model Army—and not under Charles. For the first time a monopoly of force was held by the army. And the army dictated the death of the King and Parliament—though both did their best to make any other outcome nearly impossible. But these two acts sealed the fate of dictatorship by alienating both the cities and the gentry, particularly when we add one further fact: that Cromwell did not have the heart and mind of a dictator. He was swept along by the irresistible power he had created in the army. But he would not use it as Louis was doing and, as later, Lenin and Stalin did, to liquidate dissent. Then, too, Cromwell had no successor. So almost by unanimous consent the English people found that they had had enough. Back came the Stuarts in triumph to try once again, with a stupidity which amounted to genius, to overcome the fundamental determination of British society to keep power dispersed and limited. In 1688 the Stuarts were once more rejected by force—this time for good.

The next year Parliament enacted the Bill of Rights (An Act declaring the Rights and Liberties of the Subject and settling the Succession of the Crown), the immediate ancestor of our documents of the prelude to independence. This was sent to the Prince and Princess of Orange, as the contract upon which they could and did become King William III and Queen Mary.

It wasted no time over the Rights of Man, but plunged into an indictment of James II, as less than a hundred years later the Declaration of Independence, after a slower start, indicted George III and for the same unconstitutional proceedings. It then catalogued, and again specifically, the law regarding restraints on power: It was illegal for the Crown to suspend or dispense with laws or their execution, or to levy money without grant of Parliament, or to interfere with the right to petition, or to bear arms (for Protestants), or to maintain a standing army in the country without leave of Parliament. Elections to Parliament were to be free and the debates and proceedings there not subject to question. Excessive bail or fines and cruel and unusual punishments were illegal. Jurors must be impaneled and in treason cases must be freeholders. Promises of pains or favors before conviction were illegal. Parliaments must be held frequently.

Here, as in the case of Magna Carta, no new principle was introduced, but specific rights procedurally enforceable were reiterated; and, again, the control of domestic force was dispersed among the local gentry. It has remained under local control to this day.

The heritage of the Glorious Revolution became, if anything, even more sacred in the American colonies. For, while the homeland through the first three-quarters of the century witnessed a further increase in the power of Parliament, the Americans adhered with unfailing constancy to the traditions of 1689.

Although a spirit of colonial self-reliance bordering at times on independence developed during these years, it was unconscious and well concealed beneath continuing loyalty to England. Every contest for freedom and self-government—and there were many of them between 1700 and the last great crisis of the 'sixties and 'seventies—was in reality a demand for the legal rights of Englishmen. "God be thanked, we enjoy the Liberties of England" was a frequently voiced sentiment.

The Americans demanded the same kind of limitation of power for which British subjects had been contending since the feudal era. These were not contests in the name of liberty and freedom for all mankind, but demands for specific rights and privileges, centering usually in the colonial assemblies—demands for free legislative discussion, for controls over appropriations for executive salaries, or for the exclusion of royal appointees from the lower house. All had clear precedents in the English history.

Before 1763 the colonial quest for the rights of Englishmen was entirely successful. The thirteen American legislatures, to be sure, did not possess all the privileges and power of the English Parliament, but they were capable of exercising an effective restraint on royal and imperial authority. Hence the effort of the British government at the end of the Seven Years' War to tighten imperial administration and to contract freedom of action in the colonies could not fail to arouse Americans to the controversy that led ultimately to the Declaration of Independence.

Independence was, nevertheless, not an inevitable consequence of the crisis of 1763–76. The dispute began as a demand for the same basis for taxation traditionally guaranteed by the British constitution—the old theme of the rights of Englishmen again. It was not until after ten troubled years that the colonists chose independence as a last resort. Even so, political separation from the Mother Country was largely a means of preserving traditional rights, as a cursory reading of the "new" state constitutions of the Revolutionary era will demonstrate. So we come to the ap-

The Prelude to Independence

parent paradox of Americans declaring themselves independent of Great Britain in order to preserve British liberties.

The ideas which moved the Americans during the prelude to independence still move us today at home and in one important respect in our foreign policy. In our domestic affairs the vital importance of written rights, duties, and legal procedures controlling the conduct of government and private affairs is plain enough. Perhaps we are less conscious of the diffusion of power in our society until we compare ourselves with a communist state. It is not merely the separation of the legislative, executive, and judicial powers of government, but the separation of the government and the sovereign, the official and the voter.

The idea that the voter can turn out the government and install another is held in a comparatively small part of the world and is a tremendous limitation upon power. One has to experience it to realize just how great it is. But this is not all. In our society great areas of activity are largely withdrawn from the control of government. The Church remains a competitor with all secular authority for control over conduct and thought. Vast authority over economic life is exercised by business, labor, farm, and financial organizations. The difficulty which inflation presents is not so much that the causes and remedies are obscure as that most of the forces which are producing it—for instance, private spending in replacing perfectly useful buildings, automobiles, etc., and the steady increase in prices and wages by organized business and organized labor—are as tough as the barons at Runnymede. So is entrenched local authority over education when it comes to making our schools capable of meeting the demands of our day.

In our relations with the world around us we can see—if we will only open our eyes—that one of the ideas we have discussed must be a guiding principle. Power can be limited only by counterbalancing power. Without that, treaties, international organization, and international law are of no use whatever. The possessor of unopposed or unopposable power can sweep them aside and make his will law.

With the decline in this century, and in some cases the disappearance, of the great empires which maintained a balance of power in the world during the nineteenth century and the emergence of a powerful and aggressive state in the Soviet Union, it has been and should be the policy of the United States to put restraint upon it by forming various coalitions to preserve the area of freedom. This is essential to any future expansion of the area of law in the direction of international affairs. It is also costly, risky, and often unpopular because of its demands. Often, too, it is regarded as backward looking, inflexible, and unimaginative.

But do not let us worry about that. All this was said about the great ideas and actions which made their contribution to the prelude to independence. Their authors were stating nothing new. They were preserving old rights, not asserting new ones. Their own interests were deeply involved. But in their singlemindedness, their insistence upon detail, their refusal to be put off by pernicious abstractions, their realization that what they sought for themselves must be broadened to include others and win their support, they preserved liberty and law upon this earth.

Lawyers in the Republic

"Law," said Edmund Burke, "sharpens a man's mind by narrowing it." This was witty, but only a half truth. The study and practice of law does—though not always—sharpen the mind, but not by narrowing it. Despite the metaphor of the grindstone, it does so rather by alerting it. A senior partner, who for forty years has opened possibilities of speculation to me, wondered aloud years ago why it was that the men he enjoyed talking with almost always turned out to be lawyers. It was not because he wanted to talk shop. God forbid. "The greatest bore in the world," he would say, "is a lawyer who tells you about his cases when you want to tell him about yours." No, legal shop talk is unutterably dull. Lawyers in the mass, at bar meetings for instance, are formidable in the ex-

Esquire, July, 1961, an issue devoted to the theme of "The New Sophistication."

treme; and legal humor is something to be avoided.

But it is still true that a high percentage of those whose conversation one finds stimulating and enjoyable, as my partner pointed out, are lawyers. The reason, so he thought—and I agree—is that the law is not only an intellectual pursuit, one that trains the mind to be quick and perceptive and sinks deep roots in the modes and history of human thought and experience, but it is a sophisticating pursuit. By that I mean that it tends strongly to emancipate those who follow it from their natural state of innocence and leads them into worldly knowledge—and sometimes to worldly wisdom. They are continually made aware of the complex, subtle, and varied nature of human life and human institutions. The simple blacks and whites, goods and bads, rights and wrongs of the village blacksmith under his spreading chestnut tree have to undergo considerable complicating elaboration to become useful aids to judgment in dealing with the inherent ambiguities of modern life. These ambiguities exist both in business affairs and in the relations of individuals and private organizations to that increasingly complex super-organization, the state.

Intellectual training alone is not necessarily a sophisticating experience. I am often surprised by the innocence of medical men when they venture beyond their own field into that of public affairs. Perhaps this tendency explains some of the views of the American Medical Association. May I hastily add that one would be hard put to find much sophistication in the American Bar Association's endorsement some years ago of the Bricker Amendment, which you may remember, would have limited the sovereign power of the United States in making treaties. Perhaps one could plead that this *was* some time ago and that lawyers in the mass *have* learned better. Then, too, nuclear physicists, when they burst from their laboratories after splitting the atom and became aware of the world into which they had loosed this frightful power, gave considerable evidence of both innocence of the world and hysteria as they began to learn about it.

It would, of course, be arrogant to suggest that lawyers are alone in being intellectually at home in the world of affairs. Despite the connotation given by Philistines to the word "academic," the universities are full of such people. Who would not have sat eagerly at the feet of Maynard Keynes to learn from his vast store of wisdom in the humanities, economics, and wordly affairs? If one had to name the academic disciplines most likely to produce sophisticated men, I should venture philosophy, economics, and history.

It was a philosopher who taught me an important lesson in dealing with people. We had finished a discussion in which I had analyzed a proposal put forward by another to its considerable detriment.

"You have just made a great mistake," the philosopher said, "and possibly an enemy. You have reasoned with a man who is not trained to reason, and have made him look foolish and feel frustrated. Very few people understand logic or relevance, or are governed in their thinking by either. You are trained in law; I, in philosophy. We are in a small minority. Most people associate ideas and hold them together by the strength of their wish to do so. Our colleague knows that the situation in which we find ourselves—let's call it point A—is undesirable and possibly dangerous. He looks around and sees a vision of Point B:

> . . . which seems
> To lie before us like a land of dreams,
> So various, so beautiful, so new.

But you with cold analysis and relentless logic prove that there is no road from A to B, and, that if there were, B is only a mirage which

> Hath really neither joy nor love, nor light
> Nor certitude, nor peace, nor help for pain.

You leave him robbed of hope and have stirred his resentment at you as the robber. You cannot argue him into accepting a sounder and more practicable alternative, just as—to use Justice Holmes's metaphor—'You cannot argue a man into liking a glass of beer.' You must associate your alternative with his desires. Your suggestion, let's call it point C, must be pictured with even more charms than point B. In point C the sun is brighter, the girls are prettier, the fountains run with champagne, and even the Russians have good manners and are tractable."

He was entirely right. I apologized to our colleague for my gaucheness, followed my mentor's advice, made a close and enduring friendship, and accomplished some useful results. But to return to the theme of our discussion.

There is another indication, I think, of a peculiar and special quality in the American lawyer. Alexis de Tocqueville noticed it a hundred and thirty years ago when the country was young. The study and practice of law, he thought—perhaps because he was a lawyer —produce certain habits of order, "a kind of instinctive regard for the regular connection of ideas," which make lawyers unsympathetic to unreflecting passion. Their profession, he believed, tended to make them informed, conservative, and trusted. "The government of democracy," he wrote, "is favorable to the political power of lawyers; for when the wealthy, the noble, and the prince are excluded from the government, the lawyers take possession of it, in their own right, as it were, since they are the only men of information and sagacity, beyond the sphere of the people, who can be the object of the popular choice. . . . The people in democratic states do not mistrust the members of the legal profession . . . and . . . [they] listen to them without irritation, because they do not attribute to them any sinister designs." Lawyers were, as he saw it, the essential and, happily, an accepted, stabilizing, and guiding element in the American democracy, men of "information and sagacity"—that is, sophisticated men. They made up more than a majority of the first Congress of the United States.

Sixty years later, toward the end of the century, another foreign observer, Lord Bryce, believed that the political and social position of lawyers had declined since the halcyon years. Though half of the members of Congress and the state legislatures were still lawyers, politics had become a profession in itself and power lay in the party organizations. Business was producing figures of prominence and wealth who were more the objects of popular interest and admiration than the brilliant orators of the past. And the diffusion of education had deprived the bar, the clergy, and the teachers of this once unique qualification for esteem. Nor, after some of the exploits of the "robber barons" and their legal henchmen, could it be said so flatly of lawyers that the people did not "attribute to them any sinister designs." Their position was still important, but no longer unique.

Within this century a good many American attitudes have changed. For one thing a modern de Tocqueville could not say that today "the wealthy . . . are excluded from the government." Presidents Hoover, Roosevelt and Kennedy must be classed as wealthy men, as—to name a few others—must Governors Rockefeller and Harriman of New York, and G. Mennen Williams of Michigan. But though wealth is no longer a disqualification—and may, on occasion, be a positive asset —in government, there is still room for skepticism about the value of business training as a preparation for politics. Even as conservative a man as Senator Robert A. Taft voiced this as businessmen began to take over Washington in '53: "I'm not at all sure that all these businessmen are going to work out. I don't know of any reason why success in business should mean success in public service."

History, Law, and Lawyers

At the same time the public attitude toward lawyers was also changing. Since the coming of the New Deal the view of "corporation lawyers," popularized by the muckrakers of the Progressive Era, has faded as lawyers played an increasing part in innovation in government, in the labor movement, and in the fight for the civil rights of minority and unpopular groups. Also, when the public thinks of lawyers, it thinks not only of practicing lawyers, but of teachers of law. And law schools had been rapidly gaining prestige.

The modern American law school began with Dean Langdell of Harvard, in the last quarter of the nineteenth century, and his development of the "case" system. There was nothing particularly novel about this system except in the teaching of law. As an educational method it considerably antedated the Christian era and continued in use until the "lecture" system began to sustain young minds on predigested pabulum. The case system consists of introducing students to one of the principal repositories of Anglo-American law —the actual decisions of appellate courts, arranged with regard to subject matter—and, when they have studied these raw materials, letting them discover for themselves, under the Socratic questioning of teachers able to employ this subtle method, what the case *decided*. Not what the judge *said,* but what he decided, and why. This requires precise analysis of what the issue really was, what principles of law were claimed to control its decision, and what choices, syntheses, innovations, or all three, were used by the judge in deciding the matter.

Lawyers in the Republic

Before law was taught in this way, the student read treatises on the law—Lord Coke, Littleton, or Blackstone, for instance—and learned principles. This was all very well and useful enough. But he soon discovered, when he began to practice, that in any issue worth litigating several principles might apply, and the importance of their bearing upon the decision would depend, in part, upon one's view of "the facts" and, in part, upon views about law and society held by the judge, the jury, or the community, all of which created "judgments and intuitions more subtle than any articulate major premise."

The aim of the case system was to achieve a precision, bound always to remain in large part artificial, in analysis of all these elements; and thus to relate the legal result to a specific situation, fixed in time and place. One can see at a glance that this method involves the most rigorous mental discipline. A student to be outstandingly successful must master logic, understand relevancy, and develop a capacity for long-sustained periods of concentration. The "attention time" of a successful law student or lawyer must be very long indeed. And he must understand that time spent looking at a book is not concentration. He must be vigilant, wide-awake, tensely conscious of his purpose. Justice Brandeis, who had this capacity to a marked degree, would in his later years, at the first indication of weariness, lie down on his office sofa and sleep for exactly twenty minutes. After this he was wholly refreshed.

At an earlier date, a thorough grounding in logic, that essential tool of thought, was an accepted part of education. When George Wythe's distinguished pupils came to study law with him at Williamsburg—John Marshall, Thomas Jefferson, James Monroe—we may be sure that he did not have to sharpen their minds by exercises in logic. But today this is the principal effort in nearly every first-year course. And it is the introduction to it which makes that first year so stimulating to most law students—to discover that their minds are not just sponges to soak up information to be squeezed out on the examination paper. They find minds are cutting tools to be used on tough materials to shape fascinating conceptions.

They find, too, that nearly every school of philosophy has had its counterpart in jurisprudence; that is, in a conception and rationalization of the legal system. These cover a great field, from the Greeks, who sought the source of law in reason, through those who seek it in the nature of the universe, or God's will, to Soviet writers who find it in economic determinism. Few law students penetrate far into this dim forest, where shafts of light rarely pierce. But even a short journey is useful in making one aware that most bold new conceptions for the legal order and often for governmental theory may well have a history of several centuries, if not of a millennium or more.

Underlying all legal study is something far deeper and broader. Justice Frankfurter has expressed it thus:

> No one can be a truly competent lawyer unless he is a cultivated man. . . . The best way to prepare for

the law is to come to the study of the law as a well-read person. Thus alone can one acquire the capacity to use the English language on paper and in speech and with the habits of clear thinking which only a truly liberal education can give. No less important for a lawyer is the cultivation of the imaginative faculties . . . deepen your feelings by experiencing vicariously as much as possible the wonderful mysteries of the universe. . . .

It is apparent, then, the purpose of legal education is not to "learn the law," an impossible task, but to learn to think—as Lord Chief Justice Coke put it to King James I in their long and bitter dispute over the king's claimed prerogative to take causes from the judges and decide them himself—not "by natural Reason but by the artificial Reason and Judgment of Law, which requires long Study and Experience before that a man can attain to the cognizance of it. . . ." The student acquires a knowledge of method, a knowledge of how to conduct research into the law, and of how to approach a situation in which legal factors play an important part. The actual knowledge of legal rules, and of the techniques of courtroom conduct, play a lesser part. These will come later when he practices.

It is then that as member of the bar he plays a role which is, I think, unique in this country, at least in degree. One will not find it to the same extent in Britain or on the continent.

Some years ago M. Jean Monnet, on a visit to this country to attend a dinner in honor of an American lawyer friend, made one of his rare speeches. M. Monnet, one of the brilliant men of his generation, is not well known to the American public. Even in Europe he has stayed in the background while contributing so greatly toward the integration of Western Europe through such imaginative innovations as the Schuman plan for the European Coal and Steel Community, Euratom (the joint European development of nuclear energy for peaceful purposes), the Common Market of France, Germany, Benelux, and Italy, and the European Defense Community, which France herself tragically defeated. He talked about that rare and valuable combination of qualities found in few men—the capacity for imaginative origination joined with the practical knowledge and ability to translate dreams into operating institutions. In America, throughout his own long experience in business, in two wars, and in the aftermath of the second, he had found this combination in the world of affairs chiefly among lawyers. He spoke, among many others, of the late Dwight W. Morrow, lawyer, member of the banking firm of J.P. Morgan & Co., Ambassador to Mexico, and United States Senator from New Jersey; of Mr. Donald Swatland, whose services in procurement for the Air Corps during World War II were phenomenal; and of M. Monnet's friend, the effervescent Mr. John J. McCloy, lawyer, Assistant Secretary of War in World War II, President of the World Bank, High Commissioner to the German Federal Republic, Chairman of the Chase Manhattan Bank, Presidential Adviser on Disarmament.

These men, he noted, were from firms in downtown New York and had dealt with large business and financial matters. Another lawyer of the same rare ability and the same background was the late Mr. Joseph P. Cotton, Under Secretary of State in the Hoover Administration. None of them was a court lawyer. What had impressed M. Monnet was that lawyers of this genre, by no means confined to New York, seemed peculiarly able to understand at once the uniqueness of unprecedented situations and immediately to set about devising imaginative and practical ways of dealing with them. To be able to do each of these is more unusual than appears at first glance. The unprecedented does not appear with a label around its neck announcing it to be such. This explains the tendency noted in the saying that we prepare for the next war by getting ready to fight the last. In business it explains the slowness of some executives to realize the significance of the small car, or of others to discover that the ethos of the anti-trust acts is to require competition, whatever economists may say.

Where does this practical statesmanship come from? How is it learned? In large part from the role played for nearly a half century by lawyers of the sort M. Monnet was speaking of. While familiar with the clients' affairs as few lawyers are elsewhere, they have learned to remain detached from the emotional involvement of their clients in their purposes or troubles. They must see all around situations on which they are to advise, whether they involve ambitious plans or unsought problems. More than this, I have heard both Mr. Dwight Morrow and Justice Brandeis,

in speaking of their years at the bar, say that, before
starting on a complicated and difficult negotiation,
they would spend as much time and thought on learning about and understanding the other parties' business and problems as those of their own client. Their
aim was to know more about the other fellow's business than he did, since both were persuaded that half
of the controversies arose because of the faulty understanding by businessmen, including their own clients,
of their true interests. So it should not surprise us, for
example, that of the last three Chairmen of the Board
of the United States Steel Corporation, two have been
lawyers from the same firm who had for years acted as
counsel for the corporation.

It would be untrue to attribute the capacity for legal statesmanship to the bar generally. Mr. George
Kennan complains, I think justly, of the disservice
which lawyer Secretaries of State did to American foreign policy during the years when they directed most
of our effort to the negotiation of nearly a hundred
treaties of arbitration, only two of which were ever in-
voked. He is, of course, quite right that all this mis-
guided effort sprang from a complete failure to see the
enormous threat to world stability which the Germans
were so soon to carry into action. Even after the First
World War, the realities of power were still obscured
to us by our peculiar American belief that salvation
lies in institutional mechanisms.

Candor, I believe, requires us to go further and to
concede that sometimes training and experience in the
dialectics of legal or political controversy—a most useful aid in persuading others to accept a conclusion al-

ready chosen or imposed—can be handicaps in making a choice in the first instance. Lawyers, who are habituated to having their main choices made for them by the necessities of their clients, are often at a loss when, as in government, for instance, they have wide latitude in a choice of policy.

Secretary of State Cordell Hull, for years a lawyer, judge, congressman, and briefly senator before heading the State Department, was, at first, a puzzle and then a source of delight in this matter of making a choice. After the outbreak of war in 1941, he would summon his principal assistants to a Sunday-morning conference in his office, a practice which should have been forbidden by the constitutional prohibition against "cruel and unusual punishment." During the winter the office was kept so warm that one had a half-fainting sensation of being detached from one's own body. He was sure at some point to ring for his assistant, an excellent Foreign Service Officer, Cecil Gray, known as "Joe."

When he appeared, Mr. Hull would say, "'Joe,' look at that thermometer."

"Joe" would do so, and report: "Eighty, Mr. Secretary."

"I thought so," Mr. Hull would say. "Let's have some heat."

The main business of the morning was to review events and attempt to reach some decisions on future courses. For the first few weeks I thought that the heat was affecting my mind or Mr. Hull's, as he seemed to be taking contradictory positions on the same question. But I soon discovered that this was his process of decision. He was trying out various views of the matter under discussion to find out how they went both with us and to himself. He would gradually settle on one which was more likely than not to be the decision. This method of aural thinking and analysis is a long way from the working of the more sophisticated legal minds I have been discussing. But it is not uncommon, as witness the apocryphal old lady who said:

"How can I know what I think till I hear what I say?"

I have often been asked whether there is an elite corps within the legal profession made up of Harvard Law School men who were editors of the *Law Review* and then went, after a year as law clerks to judges, to the large law firms. It was never as neat as this, but undoubtedly some years ago the statement would have contained a good deal of truth. Then the Harvard Law School was pre-eminent and service on the *Law Review* and as clerks for judges was an easy, but by no means exclusive, rule of thumb for the selection of promising material. Today there are excellent law schools in all parts of the country, or nearly all. In our own firm twenty-one law schools are represented. But prospective employers are still responsive to former law-review editors and clerks, and rightly so. They are pretty sure to have "a kind of instinctive regard for the regular connection of ideas" and to be "men of information and sagacity." One evidence of that sagacity is that the supply is kept short and the market is a seller's market. The practice of law is a highly competitive pursuit. In that pursuit ability is of great importance, but not of sole importance. Character ranks with it. It is more than likely that those graduates of the best law schools, who have excelled and won the accolades of success, have both ability and character. They are sought after by law firms. It is quite true that many of their contemporaries, less successful in the academic competition, will turn out, by the rougher judgments of practice, to be quite as good and sometimes better lawyers, and especially advocates.

So there is not an inner "elite" group at the bar in the sense of an outdated description of Balliol men at Oxford as having "a consciousness of effortless superiority." But it is true that pre-eminence at the best law schools carries with it a hallmark of no small importance.

Rereading this article, it occurs to one that some readers may get the idea that I consider cynicism to be an element of the sophistication I find among lawyers. Nothing could be more untrue. Some lawyers are, of course, cynics; the wonder is that more are not, for few professions permit such continuous observation of human folly. But it was a very great lawyer, Colonel Henry L. Stimson, who said the last word on this subject, at the end of his life in advice to younger men:

> But let them not turn aside from what they have to do, nor think that criticism excuses inaction. Let them have hope, and virtue, and let them believe in mankind and its future, for there is good as well as evil, and the man who tries to work for the good, believing in its eventual victory, while he may suffer setback and even disaster, will never know defeat. The only deadly sin I know is cynicism.

Roger Brooke Taney

Notes upon Judicial Self-Restraint

Mark Anthony is made to say by Shakespeare—

> The evil that men do lives after them,
> The good is oft interred with their bones.

The same may be said of judicial mistakes. It is the irony of fate that for three-quarters of a century the accepted conception of Roger Brooke Taney has been based upon the occasion when, yielding to the temptation, always disastrous, to save the country, he put aside the judicial self-restraint which was his great contribution to the law and custom of the Constitution.

It is of this contribution that I wish to speak. For

Address given before the Maryland Bar Association, Atlantic City, N.J., July 4, 1936.

Roger Brooke Taney

the giant stature which Taney assumes in the history
of the Supreme Court is due chiefly to his insistence
that the judge, in applying constitutional limitations,
must restrain himself and leave the maximum of freedom to those agencies of government whose actions he
is called upon to weigh. And it is an appreciation of
this view of the constitutional judge's function of
which we today stand in need.

When Taney came to the bench, John Marshall had
already established the outlines of our federal system
and the place of the Court in it. He had done so in
sweeping abstractions, in tune with the lofty philosophical approach to governmental problems which
was characteristic of his time. This very abstraction
imparted strength to his assertions, and contributed
greatly to their acceptance in a time when our government was comparatively unsettled and questions of
power might turn upon the audacity of the claimant.

But Marshall's conceptions had not yet been put to
the severe test of repeated, particularized application;
the country had hardly passed the stage when general-
izations, well nigh as broad as the Constitution itself,
would suffice to dispose of immediate issues.

As far as they had gone, Marshall's conceptions did
reflect, however, the dominant view of his generation
that the area within which governmental action
should be permitted to affect private rights was a
sharply restricted one. Indeed, it was Jefferson and not
Marshall who said that that government was best
which governed least. Laissez faire was not a party issue; the doctrine had been settled by a curious com-

bination of Adam Smith and the French Revolution. Of the principles laid down by Marshall, that which held the greatest immediate possibility for governmental restriction was contained in *Gibbons* v. *Ogden*.[1] For it was through the implied prohibition of the commerce clause that the state legislatures, which were for many generations to be the chief agencies for curbing property rights, might most sharply have been limited.

In any event, it was clear that with but little effort Marshall's decisions could have been turned into instruments for imposing upon the nation certain blunt and rigid conceptions of the rights of property, and, in the hands of a judge so inclined, the power assumed by Marshall might readily have been extended to the point where the Court would have been dictating the policy of legislation.

A further circumstance prevailing at the time of Taney's accession, when weighed against that just described, made the task of Chief Justice a most vital one. In 1828 Jackson came to power, on the crest of a movement which in the most technical sense was revolutionary. Marshall, Marshall's Court (the "Old Court" as Justice Story was nostalgically to call it), and the government of the nation theretofore had been the exclusive property of the upper classes. Between groups in those classes controversies had raged, sometimes bitterly, but, on the whole, there had been no sharp division of interest. However, with Jackson and Jacksonian Democracy there came times that made good

1. 9 Wheaton 1 (1824).

people shudder. For not only was the White House trampled with the muddy boots of the vulgar,[2] but their voices suddenly became articulate, political office fell into their hands, and they boisterously, impudently asserted a new regime claiming all power for the common man.

The philosophy of this new movement is not clearly known to us because, perhaps, it had no real philosopher. It is not unreasonable to guess that Jackson himself was an honest old Jeffersonian, and that the agrarianism of John Taylor of Caroline suited him well.[3] But it is clear that the deep passion of the whole movement was centered upon the Bank. Monopoly has always been a rabble-rousing word in our politics. Indeed the one great decision of John Marshall which was truly popular was so not because of its elaboration of the commerce power, but because it happened to strike down a monopoly.[4] And with Jacksonism there came a vituperative outburst against the Bank as the ultimate of monopolies through which, it was charged, the destiny of the masses was controlled by a corrupt coterie of financiers.

While there was nothing in Jacksonism that denied the essential thesis of laissez faire—in fact Jackson's ideal was as anarchic as Jefferson's[5]—it did look to government as the means for breaking centralized power by the simple process of withdrawing govern-

2. Bowers, *Party Battles of the Jackson Period,* p. 47.
3. Parrington, *Main Currents in American Thought,* Vol. II, pp. 145 ff.
4. Gibbons v. Ogden, supra; see Beveridge, *Life of John Marshall,* Vol. IV, pp. 445, 447.
5. Parrington, op. cit., Vol. II, p. 151.

mental support, and the support especially of the national government. And so virile was the movement that there can be little doubt that if the full implications of, let us say, the philosophy that produced the *Dartmouth College* case had been carried out, there would inevitably have been a popular collision with the Court that could have had but one event. In any case the sprawling, vociferous masses of Jacksonism were demanding that property rights, when they took the form of privilege, should not be untrammelled.

Another factor, giving point to the previous ones mentioned, entered the situation presented by Marshall's death, although it could scarcely have been appreciated at that time. The years which Taney was to serve witnessed the most profound technological and business changes in the life of the nation. The development of steam transportation—possibly the most important single episode in America's history—took place; in 1834 the first through railroad between New York and Philadelphia was opened, and twenty years later the locomotive ran uninterrupted from the Atlantic to the Mississippi. The first ocean steamship came to these shores in 1838. Immigration exceeded 100,000 a year by 1842. Gold was discovered in California in 1848, and in the same year the first general business corporation laws were enacted in New York.[6] And, as though to cap the unruly period, in 1849 the Astor Place riot occurred, one of the first times that

6. Warren, *The Supreme Court in United States History,* Vol. II, pp. 408-410.

militia reduced a mob of demonstrators with bullets.[7] In short, during this era the country was being transformed from the comparatively simple agrarian community that had borne Marshall and Madison to the plunging, reckless, complex industrialism that was already well flowered by the time the land was splashed with blood in '61. Moreover, it was during this period that the legislatures began to concern themselves with social problems. The emancipation of married women, the recognition of labor unions, prison reform, these and other measures [8] were to reflect a broadening of legislative activities into realms and for ends that had been but slightly considered during the preceding decades.

In sum: With Taney's accession the broad juridical outlines of the federal system had been sketched in lofty terms of abstract principles. But the day of philosophers had set, and the great problem facing the Court was that of giving practical, particularized content to general conceptions. Straining at old ties, there was on the political scene a new force with new values, which in its boisterous vigor demanded a reorientation in government. At the same time economic processes were to undergo far-reaching changes that made over the continent, creating unfamiliar business interests and forms, and foretelling a scope of industrial development that could not have been dreamed of in 1789. And new legislative activity developed, to herald a day when laws would trench upon the most intimate

7. Minnigerode, *The Fabulous Forties,* chap. VII.
8. Warren, op. cit., Vol. II, p. 309.

concerns of everyday life.

To a considerable extent Taney assumed his position well equipped to meet the challenge. Not all Democrats were uncouth and untrained, despite the gossip of the drawing room. When Jefferson Davis met the young lady who was to become his wife, she exclaimed, "Would you believe it, he is refined and cultivated, and yet he is a Democrat!"[9] And Taney, although a Democrat, had been one of the leaders of the talented Maryland Bar. Neither Robert Harper nor William Wirt had stood above him,[10] and when he was first proposed for the Supreme Court, before Marshall's death, the great Chief Justice indicated favor for the appointment.[11] There is no reason for surprise that his views were to be set forth with a compelling force and lawyer-like technique that hold the highest place in the Reports.

Of as much importance was Taney's understanding of, and sympathy with, the aspirations of the new political forces. Indeed he had been one of Jackson's chief lieutenants and had served his party with courage and fidelity. In his resolute discharge of Jackson's program he is said to have been fully conscious that he risked his hopes for a place on the Supreme Bench.[12] In the truest sense his was a political appointment. When his name was first presented for a place on the Court, the President was overridden by the Senate, and confirmation of his second appointment was held

9. Parrington, op. cit., Vol. II, p. 146.
10. Warren, op. cit., Vol. II, p. 154.
11. Idem. p. 260; Bowers, op. cit., p. 440.
12. Kendall, *Autobiography*, p. 386, cited in Bowers, op. cit., p. 306.

up by a bitter fight. That the fight was against Jacksonism[13] was quite proper, for there was no more staunch Jacksonian.

Contrary to the dominant trend of thought theretofore, Taney was not exclusively preoccupied with the guarantee of property rights. "While the rights of private property are sacredly guarded," he said, "we must not forget that the community also have rights, and that the happiness and well being of every citizen depends on their faithful preservation."[14] The concentration of power, the "money power" he called it, was an attempt "to destroy the spirit of freedom and manly independence in the working classes of society."[15] The granting of governmental privileges should always be made upon an exclusive consideration of the interests of the community. Shortly after his confirmation as Chief Justice he wrote to President Jackson:

> The consideration upon which alone, such peculiar privileges [corporate charters] can be granted is the expectation and prospect of promoting thereby some public interest, and it follows from these principles that in every case where it is proposed to grant or renew a charter the interests or wishes of the individuals who desire to be incorporated ought not to influence the decision of the government. The only inquiry which the constituted authorities can properly make on such

13. Warren, op. cit., Vol. II, pp. 284 ff.
14. Charles River Bridge v. Warren Bridge, 11 Peters 420, 548 (1837).
15. Warren, op. cit., Vol. II, pp. 310-311, quoting Taney to Jackson of Sept. 12, 1838.

an application is whether the charter applied for is
likely to produce any real benefit to the community,
and whether that benefit is sufficient to justify the
grant.[16]

This is not to say that Taney was radical, in the
modern sense, in regard to the rights of property. He
wrote the opinion in *Bronson* v. *Kinzie*.[17] But plainly
he understood the aspirations that were stirring humble men; he suspected the accumulation of economic
power in a few hands; and he accepted as an entirely
proper function of government the restraining of
privilege.

However a superb legal capacity and good intentions
do not suffice to explain the peculiar and permanent
contribution made by Taney to our constitutional history. The task facing the Court in 1835 was that of
making workable the juridical scheme that Marshall
had formulated. The diverse economic interests that
were rapidly developing, the new voices that were demanding attention on the political scene, the broad
acceleration of national life—all challenged the efficacy
of constitutional government, and demanded judicial
statesmanship of a high order. Taney met the test. His
decisions were to elaborate in many fields a restraint
and caution that served at once to modify the lines so
audaciously drawn by the "Old Court" and to leave to
the more elastic realm of legislative discretion the determination of much that judges before him might

16. Swisher, *Roger B. Taney*, p. 367.
17. 1 Howard 311 (1843).

have arrogated to themselves as the Constitutional Guard.

It cannot be said that the new Chief Justice advanced upon decision with any articulate political theory. He applied no touchstone of doctrine to settle questions as they *should* be settled. Rather, it was his method of approach, his respect both for the opinions of other branches of government and for the possible opinions of future generations, his technique of leaving the maximum of freedom within the constitutional imperatives which, although only partially accepted by his brethren, imparted the degree of adjustability to our constitutional structure that has preserved it until today. The recovery of his method and spirit still offers the most happy solution of the controversy which now [1936] threatens to center about the Court.

The function of formulating the great questions of policy involved in delimiting the respective spheres of the national and state governments was not, in his view, exclusively confided to the judges. His method of approach was to leave this making of policy, so far as possible, to the trial of experience and legislative judgment, reserving judicial intervention until "the angry and irritating controversies between sovereignties," [18] arising from conflicts in legislation or executive or judicial action, called for the final arbitrament provided by the Constitution. Every opportunity, he thought, should be given to solving these problems elsewhere than in the court room. "In taking jurisdic-

18. Ableman v. Booth, 21 Howard 506, 521 (1859).

tion, as the law now stands," he said in his dissent in the *Wheeling Bridge* case, "we must exercise a broad and undefinable discretion, without any certain and safe rule to guide us . . . such a discretion appears to me much more appropriately to belong to the Legislature than to the Judiciary." [19]

This attitude was not founded in any doubt of the supremacy of the national government or the right and necessity of judicial review, or in narrow provincialism, or in tenderness for the "peculiar institution" of the South; but, rather, in the intuition of the gifted ruler as to the nature and delicacy of the power he exercised.

Taney's judicial self-restraint is most familiar in his treatment of the commerce clause. In his opinion in the *License Cases,* he said:

> . . . the mere grant of power to the general government cannot, upon any just principles of construction, be construed to be an absolute prohibition to the exercise of any power over the same subject by the States. The controlling and supreme power over commerce with foreign nations and the several States is undoubtedly conferred upon Congress. Yet, in my judgment, the State may nevertheless, for the safety or convenience of trade, or for the protection of the health of its citizens, make regulations of commerce for its own ports and harbors, and for its own territory; and such regulations are valid unless they come in conflict with a law of Congress.
>
> . . . And when the validity of a State law making

19. 13 Howard 518, 587 (1852).

regulations of commerce is drawn into question in a judicial tribunal, the authority to pass it cannot be made to depend upon the motives that may be supposed to have influenced the Legislature, nor can the court inquire whether it was intended to guard the citizens of the State from pestilence and disease, or to make regulations of commerce for the interests and convenience of trade.

Upon this question the object and motive of the State are of no importance, and cannot influence the decision. It is a question of power.[20]

This view of the commerce clause contemplates a sharing of the power to determine the high question of policy whether in any situation local regulation is satisfactory or whether there is need for a uniform rule, or a different rule or no rule. Under the Taney doctrine, if Congress is satisfied to leave a matter to the states, that is an end of it. He would permit the evolution of constitutional practice by actual experience, leaving decisions in the first instance to legislatures, rather than to the *a priori* reasoning of judges. The Court would be called upon to set aside a state law only when it came into actual conflict with a law of Congress.

The case in which Taney spoke involved a regulation by a state of the sale of liquor as applied to an interstate shipment. The particular regulation was sustained, but when the question whether a state might prevent shipments of liquor into its territory was pre-

20. 5 Howard 504, 579, 583 (1847).

sented to the Court much later, the power was denied.[21] Then followed thirty years of agitation for national prohibition, the tardy attempts to repair the Court's misjudgment by the Webb-Kenyon Act[22] and the Reed Amendment,[23] and finally the Eighteenth Amendment. It is not unreasonable to believe that an acceptance of the Taney view would have spared us this whole painful and costly episode.

But the Court refused to follow Taney. Instead, it developed the now accepted rule that when the subject of regulation requires a uniform rule the federal government alone may legislate; in other fields the states may legislate until Congress acts; and in still others both governments may act. But the question in which class any particular subject matter belongs has been reserved exclusively for the decision of the judges.

The same attitude of self-restraint is shown in Taney's treatment of the right of a foreign corporation to do business.[24] Mr. Justice McKinley had held on circuit that a corporation had no existence, and could not even contract, outside the state of its creation. Webster urged upon the Court the view that corporations had a constitutional right to go into any state which local government could not deny. Here, too, Taney refused to arrogate to the Court the ultimate decision of policy. Instead he held that a rule of comity would permit a corporation, in the absence of

21. Leisy v. Hardin, 135 U. S. 100 (1890).
22. Act of March 1, 1913, c. 90, 37 Stat. 699. See Clark Distilling Co. v. Western Maryland Railway Company, 242 U. S. 311.
23. Act of March 3, 1917, c. 162, Sec. 5, 39 Stat. 1069.
24. Bank of Augusta v. Earle, 13 Peters 519 (1839).

clear prohibition by a state, to do business through its agents within the state. The power to decide whether it should be excluded, or the conditions of its admission, he left to the state. His successors, less willing to forego judicial policy-making, have narrowed the scope of this decision by superimposing the doctrine of unconstitutional conditions to the right to do business.[25]

In the *Charles River Bridge* case[26] Taney was urged with all the eloquence of Webster to hold that privileges granted by government should carry with them all the immunities from subsequent state action which would be necessary to preserve to them the full measure of their pristine strength. The argument was appealing and the weight of Story's learning and prestige was thrown to Webster's side. But the Chief Justice refused to assume the power of prescribing the rights which a legislature ought to respect. He insisted that the courts could enforce no greater rights than had been unmistakably and definitely granted and that, where there was any ambiguity, the question should be left entirely to the discretion of the legislature. Thus a franchise to operate a bridge did not perforce carry with it immunity from future destructive competition. His reasoning in deciding that charters could not by one iota be enlarged by implication is most

25. Compare, for instance, Doyle v. Continental Insurance Company, 94 U. S. 535 (1876), and Security Mutual Life Insurance Company v. Prewitt, 202 U. S. 246 (1906) with Terral v. Burke Construction Company, 257 U. S. 529 (1922). See Hale, Unconstitutional Conditions and Constitutional Rights, 35 Col. L. Rev. 321 (1935).
26. 11 Peters 420 (1837).

revealing: he could not presume the surrender of power by a sovereign state; any such view would restrain the future development of the country; and the judiciary would be plunged into a process of detailed definition and regulation of an essentially legislative character. And basic to his thought was the preservation of the essential functions of government. He wrote:

> The continued existence of a government would be of no great value, if by implications and presumptions, it was disarmed of the powers necessary to accomplish the ends of its creation, and the functions it was designed to perform, transferred to the hands of privileged corporations.[27]

Again, Taney's sound intuition led him to refuse for the Court the power to determine when one state should deliver to another a fugitive from justice and to force extradition. He was willing to leave to the governors of the states the execution of their duty under the Constitution. That they might be derelict in their duty was not a reason for the Court assuming it.

> . . . when the Constitution was framed . . . [he wrote] it was confidently believed that a sense of justice and of mutual interest would insure a faithful execution of this constitutional provision by the Executive of every State. . . .
> "But if the Governor of Ohio refuses to discharge this duty, there is no power delegated to the General Gov-

27. Id. at p. 548.

ernment, either through the Judicial Department or any other department, to use any coercive means to compel him." [28]

In one of its applications, however, the Court has fully accepted the Taney restraint.[29] *Luther* v. *Borden* [30] arose out of the disturbance of Dorr's rebellion in Rhode Island, an attempt to establish a new constitution and government in that state. The plaintiff, a partisan of the new government party, had been arrested in his house by military officers of the old government, and brought trespass. He claimed that the officers had no authority since the new government had been established by a majority of the people and should be protected by the constitutional guarantee of a republican form of government. Taney refused to go into the question of the legal authority of the government actually in power, declaring that the questions involved were political and beyond the sphere of the Court. The wisdom and authority of his restraint have never been doubted.[31] Its significance has not been fully appreciated.

28. Kentucky v. Dennison, 24 Howard 66, 109 (1860).
29. Rereading the first and penultimate sentences of this paragraph after thirty-five years shocks me by the dated and reckless character of my views. The wisdom and restraint of the Chief Justice's position as stated in 1849 were indeed respected until 1961. Then, however, in the first of the reapportionment cases a new line was taken by the Court, over the eloquent protests of Justices Frankfurter and Harlan.
30. 7 Howard 1 (1849).
31. Compare Georgia v. Stanton, 6 Wallace 50 (1867); Taylor and Marshall v. Beckham, 178 U. S. 548 (1900); Pacific States Telephone & Telegraph Company v. Oregon, 223 U. S. 118 (1912).

History, Law, and Lawyers

For the intuition which leads judges to decline to decide what they call a political question, even though it is as much bound up with the legal issue before them as many other questions which they do decide and which laymen call political or economic, is a sound caution in approaching the founts of sovereignty. When in the latter half of the fifteenth century the Duke of York laid formal claim to the crown, demanding an answer from the lords spiritual and temporal assembled in Parliament, the lords sent for the king's justices to have their advice and counsel to find all such objections as might be laid against the claim. To which the justices, after taking what we may be sure was the most earnest thought, replied that

> . . . sith this mater was betwene the Kyng and the seid Duc of York as two parties, and also it hath not be accustumed to calle the Justices to Counseill in such maters, and in especiall the mater was so high, and touched the Kyngs high estate and regalie, which is above the lawe and passed ther lernying, wherefore they durst not enter into eny communication thereof, for it perteyned to the Lordes of the Kyngs blode, and th' apparage of this his lond, to have communication and medle in such maters; and therefore they humble bysought all the Lordes, to have theym utterly excused of eny avyce or Counseill, by theym to be yeven in that matier. . . .[32]

32. Wambaugh, *Cases on Constitutional Law*, Vol. I, p. 3. Similar intuitive caution may have prompted Chief Justice Jay to decline for the Court President Washington's request for advisory opinions. (Sparks, *Writings of George Washington*, Vol. X (1836) ap-

In the fifteenth century judges who intermeddled, even upon invitation, at the very source of sovereign power might lose their heads. In the twentieth the stake is the institution of judicial review.

We have already suggested that the views of Taney are, a century later, of more than historical interest. The Court is again, as it was in his time, the center of political controversy. In both parties, as the result of recent decisions, there is talk of amending the Constitution. Some go so far as to urge a limitation upon the powers of the Court. None of these suggestions has yet been made specific. As soon as this is attempted, the difficulties will appear. Amendments designed to achieve specific purposes will be seen to effect changes far greater than anyone desires and will merely substitute new problems and uncertainties for existing ones.

The present difficulties come from judicial policy-making not necessitated by the simple language of the Constitution, but drawn from judgments and intuitions of the judges. The remedy is not to continue an unwise practice and attempt to counteract it through the dangerous and cumbersome method of amendment, but to change the practice. And the change must be by the Court itself in the attitude with which it approaches judgment upon the validity of laws. Again we turn to Taney for authority that the practice of the

---

pend. XVIII) and may have contributed to the decision of such cases as Muskrat v. United States, 219 U. S. 346; Frothingham v. Mellon, 262 U. S. 447; and New Jersey v. Sargent, 269 U. S. 328. See Finkelstein, "Judicial Self Limitation," 37 Harv. L. Rev. 338; 39 Id. 221.

Court may be subjected to critical examination without conviction of heresy. "If the judgment pronounced by the court," he wrote, "be conclusive it does not follow that the reasoning or principles which it announces in coming to its conclusions are equally binding and obligatory." [33]

In Taney's day the pressure of regulation came from the states. Today because of changed conditions the same pressure finds its outlet in congressional enactments. The Congress is quite frankly using its granted power to achieve collateral results. These attempts bring a divided response from the Court. One point of view is that the Court must examine into ultimate purposes. If it finds that Congress seeks by indirection to achieve ends which judges for *a priori* reasons of federal symmetry think or have thought should be controlled solely by the states, the Court must strike down the law, whether or not state control is possible or desired. If the country does not like this, it is said, it may change the Constitution.

The inheritors of Taney's tradition may well take a different view. They may say that the answer to all these questions is not in the simple words of the Constitution. To them it is of preeminent importance that judges should use the utmost restraint in making policy. To them it is enough—passing for a moment the due process clauses—that Congress is seeking whatever end it may be through the medium of its granted powers. They may say with Taney, "the object and motive . . . are of no importance, and cannot influence

33. Quoted by Swisher, op. cit., p. 157.

the decision. It is a question of power."[34]

True, if a conflict occurs between such a federal law and state policy however expressed, the Court must resolve it to prevent "the angry and irritating controversies between sovereignties, which in other countries have been determined by the arbitrament of force."[35] But one may feel a certain unreality in striking down a congressional exercise of a granted power, in the absence of any conflict with state policy, on the ground that in purpose and effect it invades a field reserved to the states. Judicial restraint might well lead the Court to hold its hand until an actual conflict occurs. In such a case the country would be a unit in accepting the judgment of the Court which law should prevail to preserve the federal system.

The view that Congress will usurp the functions of local government without constant discipline by the Court subjects the institution of judicial review to too great a strain by exposing it too frequently to the dangers from which the king's justices respectfully asked to be excused. Some encroachment there may be upon the "fearful symmetry" of the federal system which the "immortal hand" of Marshall framed in his basement court room. Some things may be done which appear unwise even in the long view. But no choice is possible which includes all good and avoids all harm. The choice of restraint, which entails sharing with Congress and the state legislatures the task of evolving a custom and practice, as well as a law, of the Constitu-

34. 5 Howard 583 (1847).
35. 21 Howard 521 (1859).

tion, not only assures that the path may be lighted by experience as well as logic but gives more promise than any other that the powers of the Court will survive for use when they are needed.

In the field of the due process clauses of the Fifth and Fourteenth Amendments there is equal need for judicial self-restraint. In cases of this sort the Court is asked to set aside national and state laws for reasons which in most instances defy statement convincing to the man in the street. The Court has shown a tendency to make this vague phrase—due process of law—a congeries of specific concepts drawn from the beliefs and ideology of some of the judges. Such a limitation upon a democracy, as militant as it was in Taney's day, cannot be reasonably expected to endure. And little is gained by the interpretation that the clause prohibits what a majority of the judges find to be arbitrary or unreasonable. Anything with which we strongly disagree seems unreasonable and arbitrary.

Again, what is needed is not a rule but a method of approach. The due process clause conceived as a method of sober appeal to better judgment has a real function and utility. But the appeal must be successful. If it fails, it is worse than useless, as the last attempt testifies.[36] Justice Holmes used to tell a story of going as a young man to Emerson with an essay he had written on Plato. After reading it, Emerson's only com-

36. Morehead v. Tipoldo, 80 L. Ed. 921, decided June 1, 1936; see Mr. Landon's telegram of June 11, 1936, to the Republican Convention, New York Times, June 12, 1936, p. 1; Democratic Platform, 1936, "The Constitution."

ment was, "My boy, when you strike at a king, you must kill him."

If the Court strikes at a law with the due process clause it must kill it. It must be able to convince the great majority of press and people by compelling analysis in terms generally accepted that the law was arbitrary. If judges cannot convince their brethren, they might well ponder the implications of their failure. Judges, as Justice Holmes has said, "need something of Mephistopheles." They "too need education in the obvious." [37]

Taney's great service was to teach the lesson of self-restraint. His task came to an end in a setting of unequalled tragedy. Appomattox was casting its inevitable shadow over fields drenched in blood. His son-in-law was with the forces of the Confederacy. Old, lonely, broken in body and spirit, he was hated and vilified by men whose passions were fanned by war and whose pens were dipped in gall. He died in October, 1864. Of official Washington only the President and two members of the Cabinet would attend the brief service held there. When his body was brought back to rest in his native state his spirit might well have said in the words of Wolsey:

> An old man, broken with the storms of state,
> Is come to lay his weary bones among ye.
> Give him a little earth for charity.

His Maryland has given him a little earth, and not

37. *Collected Legal Papers*, p. 295.

in charity but honor. Indeed, he sits today before the old State House, first in Maryland's affection, his brooding figure the cynosure of awe and veneration. Beyond his homeland, prejudice and calumny have beat upon him with a blind relentlessness scarce equalled in our history. Yet, in the musty pages of the Reports, his teachings have been preserved and today those who anxiously defend our constitutional order will do well to scan with care the records of his thought. For they disclose that high humility without which judicial power must ultimately fail.

The Arrogance of International Lawyers

Five years ago I was bold enough to scold a meeting of this sort about what I call the arrogance that international law seems to instill in its addicts. To be sure, law in general does this to lawyers in general. One can be tolerantly amused at the veneration which craftsmen in any craft have for the materials of their craft. The cobbler murmurs, "There's nothing like leather!" But he is too modest to envision as man's highest earthly condition the Rule of Leather. Yet the lawyer does not blush to proclaim it to be the Rule of Law. As he describes it, the rule of law seems to be governance by disembodied principle without the intervention of human hand or voice. Even his own not

Address given before the Section of International and Comparative Law of the American Bar Association, Washington, D. C., May 24, 1968. Published in *International Lawyer*, vol. 2, No. 4 (July, 1968).

unimportant role at the bar and on the bench the lawyer turns into the mere voice of the oracle inspired by the Law Principle itself. This miracle finds its most mystical expression in the doctrine of Natural Law, which makes it the efflux of the universe, flowing forth from the Godhead. The disciple of Natural Law seemed to Justice Holmes like the knight of romance to whom it was not enough that you agreed that his lady was a very nice girl. If you did not admit that she was the best that God ever made or would make, you must fight. Ordinary lawyers, who work around the temple of Apollo feeding the oracle questions, some of which are loaded, arguing with it and among themselves, "cussing" its pronouncements that go against them, take a more earthy view of law. When former Justice (as he was then) Charles Evans Hughes bluntly—and, perhaps, too "Delphically"—said that the Constitution is what the Supreme Court says it is, the lawyers were not too shocked, although they pretended that they were.

Those who devote themselves to international relations in foreign offices at what is disparagingly called "the working level" are understandably and wisely reticent about the role of law. This, however, is not true of academicians who write about it and teach it. Undeterred by the discipline of adversary procedure or by the test of judgment in contested application, motivated by the highest principles and often spurred by a gift for imaginative rhetoric, some of them recall Disraeli's description of Gladstone as "intoxicated by the exuberance of his own verbosity." I hasten to add that it was the Bar Association *en masse,* and not the

International and Comparative Law Section of it, that voiced the most delusive of all slogans—"World peace through world law."

Those of whom I complain are not the peddlers of spurious panaceas for peace, not those who are over-impressed with the role of international law, but those who would impose upon states in the name of law their own subjective conceptions of justice. As is so often the case with the righteous, deeply convinced of the righteousness of their cause, their impulse is to "snatch the knotted cords from the hand of God and deal out murderous blows." These blows are usually directed against the weak by suborning the subjectivities of the strong. This process also furnishes the fig leaf of legal respectability for otherwise naked aggression.

Such support was given to the action of the United Nations Security Council in calling for economic sanctions against Rhodesia and to the attacks upon the World Court's decision dismissing the complaint in the Southwest Africa case. The viciousness of the substitution of the subjective conception of justice for law in these instances is that in both cases it provides means for collective aggression, in both it degrades international adjudication, and in both it departs from the basic conception of international law. This is that it is inter *national,* between sovereign states, based upon accepted practices and agreements of sovereigns. In this latter respect it differs basically from the law taught by the international lawyers' other academic colleagues. To strike at this concept of agreed limitations on sovereignty is to strike at confidence in judicial honesty and restraint, which alone can lead to the slow development of international law from its primitive state.

It will surprise some of my fellow citizens, though hardly anyone here today, to be told that the United States is engaged in an international conspiracy, instigated by Britain, and blessed by the United Nations, to overthrow the government of a country that has done us no harm and threatens no one. This is barefaced aggression, unprovoked and unjustified by a single legal or moral principle.

The charge that Britain brings against Rhodesians is one that George III once brought against Americans and sought unsuccessfully to enforce by arms. It was that the Colonies felt it necessary, as Mr. Jefferson put it, "to dissolve the political bands which [had] connected them with another [people], and to assume among the powers of the earth, the separate and equal station to which the Laws of Nature and of Nature's God entitle them." However, two academics writing in the *American Journal of International Law* have taken a quite different view. They say:

> . . . In the most fundamental sense, the assertion of independence at a time and by means which the authoritative organs of the international community had decided would precipitate a threat to the peace of the surrounding region and the world was an act of irresponsibility in violation of the most basic policies of the Charter for the maintenance of international order.[1]

1. Myres S. McDougal and W. Michael Reisman, "Rhodesia and the United Nations: The Lawfulness of International Concern," 62 *A.J.I.L.* 1, tp. 12 (1968).

The Arrogance of International Lawyers

Where authorities differ so widely further inquiry and judgment are indicated.

In the first place, was independence so broad a step for Rhodesia to take? While Britain had asserted sovereignty over the Rhodesian countryside since the latter part of the last century when Cecil Rhodes started developing it, Whitehall had never administered government there, nor provided funds or forces for its defense. All this had been done locally, first under the British South Africa Company chartered to Cecil Rhodes and his associates, and after 1923 under the Constitution of that date, established after the electorate had voted for self-government as against incorporation in the Union of South Africa. In fact, so self-governing was Rhodesia that between 1935 and 1953 (the beginning of the Federation) the Rhodesian Prime Minister sat as an equal in the meetings of Prime Ministers, first of the Empire and later of the Commonwealth. The Prime Minister of the Federation (with Nyasaland and Northern Rhodesia) took his place until its dissolution in 1964. Thereafter the Prime Ministers of her two associates, now independent states, sat, but Rhodesia's was excluded because of the dispute which then arose.

Turning to this dispute and the circumstances of the Rhodesian assertion of independence, that country had had since the beginning of its history an electorate based on adult male suffrage, later extended to women, with modest literacy and property requirements. These qualifications are those adopted in this and other countries during early stages of representative government by a people among whom education was the exception, and experience, cultural or otherwise, was unequal. When white settlement began in 1890, Rhodesia was sparsely populated by very primitive people. The great bulk of its present population, white and black, has immigrated since then, attracted by opportunity and security of life and property available there. The Rhodesian Constitutional Commission was well aware of this situation:

> . . . the Shona, the Ndebele and the Europeans were all in turn [im]migrants, conquerors and settlers and all now know no other home. Thus they have established for themselves and their successors the right to remain in the country in perpetuity, a right which they have every intention of exercising.
>
> . . . .
>
> . . . For the[se] reasons . . . Rhodesia is the permanent and rightful home of peoples of different origins and backgrounds, and does not belong to one race or ethnic group alone. . . .[2]

What did the Commission see as the end of the matter? A progressive extension of the franchise, but not majority rule. "For a time which cannot be measured by clock or calendar," Europeans would exercise the more authoritative voice at national government level, and Africans would have a voice that must be allowed increasing, but not limitless, power. The ultimate solution recommended was based on racial parity of

2. *Report of the Constitutional Commission, 1968* (Government Printer, Salisbury, Rhodesia), Chapter 2, p. 10.

The Arrogance of International Lawyers

representation as most likely to produce immediate and long-term confidence and stability. This was not everyone's cup of tea; neither was it everyone's business; nor was it *apartheid*. It was a matter relating solely to the internal affairs of Rhodesia—in which the United Nations was forbidden by its Charter to meddle—and to the political relation between Rhodesia and the United Kingdom. When the latter sought to impose a majority rule, in time measured by the calendar, Rhodesia severed the bands that bound them.

It was this act and Rhodesia's assumption, among the powers of the earth, of the separate and equal station to which the Laws of Nature and of Nature's God entitled her which the General Assembly and the Security Council said created a situation that threatened the peace. While Rhodesia threatened no one, the idea was that her independence, "if continued in time," would disturb the peace because, apparently, someone would attempt to terminate it, because of disapproval of Rhodesia's long-established internal legislation on suffrage. The General Assembly spelled this out in its Resolution of November 5, 1965, when it "reaffirm[ed] the right of the people of Southern Rhodesia to freedom and independence [—the very thing which was now threatening the peace—] and recogniz[ed] the legitimacy of their struggle for the enjoyment of their rights." What sort of rights? Their rights as set forth in the Charter of the United Nations, the Universal Declaration on Human Rights, and the Declaration on the Granting of Independence to Colonial Countries and Peoples. [The resolution went on that the United Nations "solemnly warn[ed] the present authorities in Southern Rhodesia and the United Kingdom of Great Britain and Northern Ireland, in its capacity of administering Power, that the United Nations will oppose any declaration of independence which is not based on universal adult suffrage."][3]

How fortunate were the American colonies to have no United Nations to confront in 1776! I need hardly remind you that our Constitution had nothing to say about adult universal suffrage but did have a few pregnant paragraphs continuing the institution of slavery.[4]

Of course, no one in the United Nations really believed that Britain, which had been handing out independence in wholesale lots, would fight Rhodesia, or that any African state would take on the prickly job.

Perhaps I might pause for a moment to remind you of the present situation. As everybody knew, this blockade of Rhodesia has not worked. Therefore, Her Majesty's Government, in accordance with that universal principle which seems to instigate all fanatics that one must redouble effort on finding oneself on the wrong road, has asked the United Nations to extend the blockade and our African friends have raised their cry that the British should come out of the bushes and gain enough courage to fight Rhodesia by arms. The point I am making here is that this highly theoretical and imaginative threat was not posed *by* Rhodesia but *against* Rhodesia. From this premise only the most Humpty-Dumpty reasoning could move to the

---

3. General Assembly Resolution No. 2022, 60 *A.J.I.L.* 922-23.
4. U.S. Constitution, Art. I, §§ 2 (clause 3) and 9 (clause 1); Article IV, § 2 (clause 3).

conclusion that Rhodesia should be punished by international action aimed at overthrowing her government and ending her independence. The reasoning provided by academic authority is hardly less curious. Here it is:

> . . . In the contemporary intensely interdependent world, peoples interact not merely through the modalities of collaborative or combative operations but also through shared subjectivities—not merely through the physical movements of goods and services or exercises with armaments, but also through communications in which they simply take each other into account. . . . Much more important than the physical movements are the communications which people make to each other. In the case of Rhodesia, the other peoples of Africa have regarded themselves as affected by the authoritarian and racist policies of the Rhodesian elites. . . .[5]

In simpler and nonpejorative terms, they do not like Rhodesia's elective system. Subjectivity means the quality or condition of viewing things exclusively through the medium of one's own mind or individuality; the condition of being absorbed in one's personal feelings, thoughts, concerns, etc. The term also means personal bias, emotional predisposition, the substitution of perception for reality, etc. The authors may mean any or all of those senses. But the point is that what we have here is the idea that law is only a mirror of the beholder's emotional condition at the moment.

5. McDougal and Reisman, *loc. cit.,* pp. 1, 12.

History, Law, and Lawyers

Consider a situation which wounds shared subjectivities of a wholly different nature and ones with which we may be less in sympathy. Within the month the nations of Eastern Europe have met in Moscow to consider their shared dislike of what they regard as the deviationist, antidemocratic, indeed, bourgeois policies of the Czechoslovakian elites in permitting a modicum of personal liberty in that country. Rumor even carries reports of Soviet troop movements near the Czech border. Suppose that, instead of repeating its armed interventionist tactics in Hungary in 1956, the Soviet Union should appeal to the Security Council to stop this Czech assault on the shared subjectivities of communist states. I suppose that the authors would expect it to direct us all to cease building bridges to the East and refurbish our embargoes against trade with a renegade communist state.

Consider, too, our own parlous position in the face of this doctrine. Does any country in the world so widely offend shared subjectivities as we do? General de Gaulle, Mao Tse-tung, Ho Chi Minh, Mrs. Gandhi, Castro, the Arabs, even the South Vietnamese have all suffered. And what about our own subjectivities should our own brain child, the United Nations, expound on what we had done to theirs. Somehow this romantic interpretation of the Charter does not make it read like the last best hope for peace on earth.

Nevertheless, ridiculous as it appears on analysis, much as it recalls Cicero's observation that there is nothing so absurd but some philosopher has said it, the fact remains that it rationalizes an attempt to over-

164

throw a government that has done us no harm and threatens no harm to any state. Is participation in such an assault desirable foreign policy? Is this cabal what Mr. Hull thought was being prepared at Dumbarton Oaks or what the Senate almost unanimously ratified?

Of course, clever men will attempt to use any instrument to accomplish indirectly what they cannot do directly; but we should have known better than to agree to it had we not been bemused by substituting ideas that appealed to us as ethical for the plain engagements of sovereign states. In the Charter the subscribing sovereigns undertook not to use force as an instrument of policy in their international relations. By a process that cannot be dignified as reasoning, force applied against another state has now been equated with the failure to adopt internally the principle of universal suffrage plus the egalitarian doctrine of equally weighted votes as announced by the Supreme Court of the United States in *Baker* v. *Carr*. And this—mark you!—is only the first application of that new doctrine of international lawyers—the sovereign equality of shared subjectivities.

This doctrine is allied in its harmful and disruptive potentialities with the doctrine of liability without injury, averted only by the casting vote of the President of the World Court in the decision of the Southwest Africa case. An analogy to this case would have been an original action, in the Supreme Court of the United States, say by the State of Michigan, activated by the policies of its former governor in his State Department days, against the State of Virginia to correct the school situation once said to prevail in King William County. If the Court had found that neither the State of Michigan nor any of its citizens had been injured, its precedents (which it might or might not have followed) would have required it to dismiss the case for want of jurisdiction. This is what the World Court found and did. The wounding of shared subjectivities would, of course, furnish jurisdiction for the Court on the same reasoning as for the Security Council.

Contemplating the possibilities, I am moved to salute the shade of Senator Tom Connally and thank him for his reservation, which at the time I regretted, providing that our acceptance of the World Court's jurisdiction should not apply to disputes with regard to matters that are essentially within the domestic jurisdiction of the United States as determined by the United States.

One of the troubles of the troubled age in which we live is that too many people are trying to achieve harmony of interest by forcing everyone to harmonize with them. Conscience used to be an inner voice of self-discipline; now it is a clarion urge to discipline others. It took a long time to develop the international precept that peace would be furthered by governments' having respect for each other's autonomy. That should apply to them when acting in concert. This is the notion embedded in Paragraph 7 of Article 2 of the Charter. Whatever mistakes they may otherwise have made, the draftsmen of the Charter, at least, did not intend to open the way for endless conflict through unbridled impulses to reform. The new romantic impulse is to overthrow that wise inhibition in favor of a compulsion to reshape the world to fit all sorts of shared subjectivities.

Another thought also occurs. Perhaps, if the meek are to inherit the earth, they might consider adding a clause to the litany. It could follow "From all blindness of heart; from pride, vainglory, and hypocrisy; from envy, hatred, and malice, and all uncharitableness" and would add "and from the United Nations Charter as distorted by professors of international law,

Good Lord, deliver us."

Part Four ⫷

Little for Your Comfort

Nunc Dimittis

A day of national mourning, such as this is, brings to our minds and gives us an opportunity to remind ourselves of the words of John Donne: "No man is an island entire of itself . . . Any man's death diminishes me . . . therefore, never send to know for whom the bell tolls; it tolls for thee." Yet another death has diminished our country and all of us. And the bell tolls for us.

It is, I think, the insight of military ritual that requires troops leaving a graveside to leave it to the music of a quickstep. Those of you who have read the correspondence between those two great old men of American history, John Adams and Thomas Jeffer-

On June 9, 1968, on the occasion of Exeter's 187th Commencement, the Honorable Dean Acheson, grandfather of David C. Acheson, a member of the graduating class, delivered the Commencement address. It was but a few days after the death of Senator Robert F. Kennedy.

son, written after they had been reconciled by the good offices of Dr. Rush, remember their discussion about the emotion of mourning, sorrow, and regret. They find this to be the most debilitating of all the emotions, and the least useful in human life. They conclude that it should be ended quickly—and ended by a return to the duties of life.

I like a story which is told about Col. Abraham Davenport, one of our early Yale graduates and the great-grandson of a founder of New Haven. May 19, 1780, was in central Connecticut a day of awful memory. At noon the sky was as black as midnight. The House of Representatives, unable to transact business, was adjourned and the members fled into the streets to join there the throngs who were praying for salvation. In the Council of Safety, the Upper House of the Connecticut Legislature, the motion to adjourn was made. Whereupon, Col. Davenport asked for and received recognition. His words were transcribed and here they are: "The day of judgment is either approaching or it is not. If it is not, there is no cause for adjournment. If it is, I choose to be found doing my duty. I wish, therefore, that candles may be brought." Today, perhaps we, too, need candles to be brought in order that we may be found doing our duty, and all the more so since the surrounding gloom seems to have engulfed the institutions of learning to which all of you are now going.

It has occurred to me to wonder in the last few months whether at this time of Commencement, university presidents are more pleased by the fact that they are losing a class than by the expectation that they will soon gain one. Perhaps there ought to be a *Nunc Dimittis* written for college graduations: "Lord, now lettest thou these students depart in peace, according to our word."

Looking at you with the freshness of youth still upon you, it is hard for me to believe that you have within you the seeds of that delinquency which so marks your future classmates. Within the month, *The New York Times* has informed us that large numbers of what it calls "nominally educated young" have no stake in Western civilization that they know of. This report, if true, suggests that perhaps their education has indeed been nominal. A report in *The Washington Post* carries the matter further. It says: "A small group of students are so disillusioned with the United States that they want to destroy the existing institutions although they have nothing to offer in their place. A far larger number," it goes on, "are so unhappy with particular aspects of society or of education that they are willing (or naive enough) to join the game. . . . These students think that universities are badly administered and irrelevant to the needs of students. . . . They think the nation is wrong in some of its policies and has put its priorities on the wrong programs. They find rightly, or wrongly, that the world they are inheriting is a miserable one, and they blame their parents for its condition."

Perhaps we should first clear up this last canard, lest by implication it be thought to apply to your parents. Now, I have observed that generation for some time.

Little for Your Comfort

Indeed, I am somewhat closer than an observer to two of its members, and I wish to assure you on solemn oath before this audience that they were not responsible for either the first or the Second World War, nor did they bring on the cold war, nor did they blight the promise of the Emancipation Proclamation, nor otherwise are they responsible for your miserable condition except, possibly, the inadequacy of your allowances. Now do not let what I say allow you to become permissive towards your parents; they need a strong hand from you to prepare them for what undoubtedly lies ahead of them. If there is blame to be handed out for the condition of the world, I have already received a fair share of it. This, however, appears to be an occupational hazard of an office I once held, or else it is mere flattery on the part of my enemies.

Doubtless, many students do believe, as many voters do also, that the nation has been wrong in some of its programs and some of its priorities. In fact, this idea has crossed my mind once or twice. But the responsibilities of the universities for these governmental decisions has been exaggerated by Mr. Arthur Schlesinger, Jr. It has never seemed to disgruntled adults a good idea to throw in their jobs or get fired from them in order to register their disapproval of national policies either to the Congress or to one who is known as "that man in the White House."

What, however, shall we think of the statement that a large group of students are disenchanted and believe that universities are badly administered and are irrelevant to their needs? I have no doubt that some think this, and possibly they have an idea of what their needs are. But just how they know what their needs are has never been very clear to me. Possibly some faculty members agree with them. But I am inclined to believe that those faculty members are the ones who consider that they have not received the recognition to which, in Mr. Jefferson's phrase, they thought nature and nature's God, perhaps, entitled them. You are closer to Cicero than I am, and you will remember where he said: *"Nihil tam absurde dici potest quod non dicatur ab aliquo philosophorum*—nothing is so absurd but what some philosopher has said it." The point is, not what is believed, but what is true.

For a good many years—more than thirty now—I have been visiting colleges and talking with college students all over the United States. I have even had a small part in the administration of one university. I doubt whether an experienced educator would quarrel with the statement that today higher education in this country is the best that exists, or that has ever existed, for the mass education of a great democracy, and for specialized training in the professions and in advanced research. Anyone who knows the universities knows a thousand ways in which they can be improved, and about nine hundred of these require mostly more money—the rest require some diminution of the old Adam and perhaps a little of the young Eve.

In Europe sound complaint can be made against time-encrusted universities and methods of education, both by students from that section of the population which is newly coming to higher education and by the new democracies which the old universities must now serve. They have a proud history. They have created great scientists and great humanists. But the faculties, which have so long dominated them, must now adjust to a new task. They must heed the words of Lord Sherbrooke, who after the passage of the Reform Bill of 1867 said, "Now, we must educate our masters."

Some idea of the extent of this task lies in a startling statistic. The percentage of those completing high school and going on to higher education in the most deprived group of our society, which is Negro youth, is larger than the percentage of all young people in Western Europe who do the same.

Whatever may be believed, American colleges and universities are not badly managed, and they are not irrelevant to the needs of their students. Far more is eagerly and devotedly offered than the most voracious student can consume. For the most part, upon the testimony of scores of faculty members and hundreds of students, particularly in the great stretches of this country between the Alleghenies and the Rockies, these offerings are being eagerly received.

I have often been reminded going about this country of a visit my wife and I paid some years ago to a country in southeast Asia, where the only institution in the whole country beyond the pagoda schools was a sort of coeducational junior college, which was supposed to teach the future teachers. A gray-haired, kindly Quaker lady was showing us around that institution, a most primitive one where all the classes recited in unison as they did two hundred years ago in this country. I asked her about her disciplinary problems, and she said very sadly that she wished she had more. I remarked that this was not the common complaint of deans, and she said even more sadly that for her students the alternative to successful graduation was the paddy field.

I have heard that for the more serious of our students the alternative in terms of American life is not very dissimilar. The difference between successfully completing higher education and not completing it is not exactly the paddy field, but in comparative terms you will understand what I mean.

Today, university and college authorities are drawing students into the administration of their institutions of learning. Not only in matters of student government but, also, in matters which I doubt that they are qualified to perform, such as the curriculum and the promotion or advancement of faculty members. As I recall my youth, which seems a million years away, I cannot recall that we ever had this passion for responsibility. I may be wrong, but I recall that we were quite willing to leave discipline to the deans and to the campus cops, and we intervened only when it seemed possible to provide a classmate who was in trouble with at least a semibelievable alibi.

Even the rules about the presence of females in dormitories—which, as I recall it, were on the same principle employed by a classmate in choosing his courses, "none above the first floor and none after one o'clock" —did not greatly disturb us. To some they seemed to infringe the fundamental rights of man and to the dean they seemed to embody a great moral issue. The first we regarded as an overstatement. As to the moral issue, we agreed with the view of a lady in our community in Maryland who immortalized herself by insisting that some moral issues were as important as real issues. This, however, did not seem to us to be one of those.

The attitude of an English college in a university of great antiquity, where I lectured some years ago, toward undergraduate behavior seemed to me highly sophisticated. At the opening of term the Provost told the students that the college had no rules at all. He said that he thought it would be obvious to them that anyone who did not wish to pursue study, and anyone who persistently annoyed his neighbors, would make both himself and them much happier if he decided to live elsewhere. This seemed to be a very workable way to approach the whole matter of conduct.

But if the malaise in the universities does not spring from their deficiencies or from a tendency to exclude students from participation in their operation, where shall we look for it? The article in the *Times* that I have quoted suggests that it originates in an aberration in student values. On campus, the editorial writer tells us, "The big man is the loser, the outcast, the four-letter varsity intransigent. . . . Protest," he goes on, "can provide an esthetic élan. . . . Our society," he concludes, "does not now offer any genuine moral outlet for physical courage." This, I suggest, combines error with oversimplification and misreading of a serious problem.

Nunc Dimittis

Those who are close to recent publicized trouble in an important university tell me that it was instigated by three small and well-disciplined ideological groups and participated in by a fourth and wholly undisciplined group, which was looking merely for a frolic and a fight. A Maoist and a Stalinist group were out to prepare for the overthrow of the *existing* order; an anarchist group was out to overthrow *all* order. None of these had any interest whatever in any issue with the university; they wanted solely to provoke police intervention, disorder if possible, and a wider conflict involving more students. When the disciplined *agents provocateurs* meekly withdrew before superior police power, the fourth group, originally against the others, was left alone confronting the police. In true Mack Sennett comedy style, the police believed that the adventure-seekers were the enemy and vice versa; whereupon a rough and bloody battle ensued, which as usual enlisted general student sympathy for the surprised and not over-bright victims of alleged police brutality.

Two morals stand out from this: One is that things are not what they seem; the other is to stay out of physical confrontation when *both* town *and* gown are arrayed against you.

The third might be that students of sense and judgment should be aware that their role in the United States today is not to emulate students in warmer and less sophisticated environments by attempting to stir up revolution or by fighting with the police, but to realize that they do not go to a university to anticipate their hour of responsibility by taking over its adminis-

tration. Their purpose and role is to acquire competence—competence to discharge their responsibility
when their hour strikes. Lest you dismiss this thought
as too conservative, let me cite a distinguished revolutionary leader in support of it. He has just been our
nation's guest in Washington. This is President Habib
Bourguiba of Tunisia.

Last year he responded to a memorial addressed to
him by Tunisian students assembled in their Congress.
In replying he said, somewhat drily, that its contents
showed that they had acted more as a political group
than a professional body. They dealt, he said, "with
the most varied international problems." The problems of all continents, he pointed out, were mentioned.
The only problems that were not discussed were those
that concerned Tunisian students. This led him to
assume, or would have led him to assume, that they
had no problems, if he had not been busily engaged
for the past year in trying to resolve them. In his own
student days, he went on, his "primary concern was
to study, to learn, and to amass information." "Before
adopting political positions," he said, "or publishing
articles in newspapers, I wanted to acquire sufficient
baggage to be able to form a sound judgment. In order
to launch the struggle [for independence], I had first
of all to pursue my effort of investigation and reflec-
tion as far as possible."

Now, this is good common sense. A student's job is
"to acquire sufficient baggage to be able to form a
sound judgment," not to check what baggage and judgment he has in order to pursue causes or to protest

that the world is not a better place than it is. Furthermore, there is a better than even chance that he will find more "esthetic élan" in becoming intellectually competent than in voicing protest and that, contrary to the supposed undergraduate belief (which I doubt exists), our society will offer plenty of genuine moral outlet for all the physical courage that one can muster. It has been so over the two generations that have preceded yours. My wish for your future would be rather less call for courage, physical and moral, than I see as probable in the years before you.

But, let me leave you on a note of hope by assuring you that graduation speakers' visions of the future are even more fallible than the general average of vision in the community. When I was in your position fifty-seven years ago, nothing could have appeared more stable and secure than the world we had inherited from the nineteenth century. The Peace Palace at The Hague was nearing completion. War had been made impossible due to international interdependence. The United States was bursting with expansion and prosperity. For graduates of schools like yours and mine the chief danger would be expanding complacency and expanding waistcoats. Before we were out of college the whole world order and the great empires that supported it had gone to irretrievable ruin and destruction. Insecurity and disorder, which had been the common lot of mankind for all recorded history, had taken its place.

The bright promises of a world of *Locksley Hall* proved to be illusions. I have no more faith in the dire prediction of the Götterdämmerung that awaits you. Despite the new school of despair, the work of the past twenty-five years has not been all futile and stupid. A new Phoenix world has arisen from the old. Your inheritance is not ashes and tears, but material worthy of a sculptor, or better still a gardener who can mold the living forces of nature into beauty and sustenance. The young people of today, not as I read about them, but as I know them, have the stuff to bring forth the world of the twenty-first century. In this task protest is a waste of time; idealism is not enough. What is essential is what you are going on to attain. "Brave men," it has been written, "are not uncommon in any system, but there is a tendency in most systems to make courage and openness of mind to the significant facts mutually exclusive." You have courage. You have intelligence. You are going on to attain competence. We wish you good luck all the way.

The Changing American Scene

*And Its Implications
for Our Well-Being*

Lord Kenneth Clark has described a period strikingly similar to our own as a time of "Protest and Communication." [1] He was referring to the Reformation in sixteenth-century Europe. Then, while a new world was in process of discovery and new horizons were unfolding, a novel method of communication fanned long-dormant embers of protest into flames that destroyed the unity of Christendom and the very conception of universal authority. The protest of the fifteenth century was prelude to the destruction of the Thirty Years' War in the seventeenth, unequalled

Address given at the United States Air University, Maxwell Air Force Base, Alabama, May 13, 1970.

1. Kenneth Clark, *Civilisation* (New York: Harper & Row, 1969), p. 139.

since barbarian invasion had put an end to the *Pax Romana*.

The novel method of communication was the printing press. "People used to think of the invention of printing," observed Lord Clark, "as the linchpin in the history of civilisation. Well, fifth-century Greece and twelfth-century Chartres, and fifteenth-century Florence got on very well without it—and who shall say that they were less civilised than we are? Still, on balance, I suppose that printing has done more good than harm."

Can one say as much of radio and television, which are dominating our age? Whatever the answer, the question is probably the wrong one. If we ask instead whether the impact of radio and television on our age is comparable to that of printing on the sixteenth century, the answer must be: certainly—but far greater in affecting the pace and direction of change. Surely the fact that the Korean War was the last to be reported mainly by press and the Vietnamese the first to come to the viewer directly through television has had a great deal to do with the change in the public attitude between the two. Can one doubt that, had General Grant's Wilderness Campaign and the fighting from Somme through Passchendale been seen on television, the problems of all leaders, but especially those of Presidents Lincoln and Wilson, would have been even more difficult than they were and vastly different?

In the sixteenth century the printed word needed nearly a hundred years to fan protest to effective and destructive action. The real and alleged causes of protest had long been present. Doctrinal and organizational conflicts were not new within the universal church. Political unease between the Emperor and the Pope and between both and the great feudal lords had laid fuel for the kindling despite the removal of restless spirits by the crusades. Protest against the harshness of the feudal system had already burst into violence with the Peasants' Revolt and its bloody suppression. Even so, criticism of religious and political authority was carried by a slow, small current to a few selected segments of society, and addressed to an educated elite. Today, in sharp contrast, an insistent torrent of information, misinformation, and opinion on all subjects overwhelms our society for lack of historical perspective and a prevailing sense of values necessary to cope with it. This lack is a consequence of the pace of change. In my lifetime the population of our country has more than trebled. By the end of the century it will increase further by an amount equal to the combined populations of Britain and France. An estimated 88 percent of our people will live in cities of over 100,000 inhabitants. The strides in science and technology surpass all achieved between the origin of the wheel and the nineteenth century. The increase of material production over only the past twenty years has been so great as to produce an environmental crisis of the basic elements of life itself—air, water, and the supporting earth.

Adjustment to the pace of change is quite as upsetting as to change itself. Over many millennia women have been struggling to overcome restraints variously attributed to men and biology. In the past century the rate of change in their status has been bewildering. Economic pressures, education, and medical science have all contributed to it. Its effect on the unit basically affecting contemporary culture, discipline, and ethical standards—the family—has been enormous.

All these changes have cumulatively accentuated another apparently new, but actually very old and always disturbing, phenomenon—the conflict of generations. To both Plato and Aristotle, revolt for its own sake by the young against the system and establishment of their elders—whatever it might be—provided the chief periodical cause of social change. It had no consistent purpose or effect; merely to change the status quo. Latterly it has been observed that this revolt has occurred only during static social periods when the younger generation found no escape from the geographic or other limitations of their elders' society. When, however, new fields or opportunities were opened by new discoveries, adventurous youth flocked off to new fields to make their own mistakes with joyous unrestraint. Even in static periods, it has been pointed out, those who protested were rarely themselves oppressed, but were more affluent youth, who might be called parasitic protestants. Thus, in Europe of 1848 middle-class and well-to-do students were championing working-class grievances; and in Russia, at the turn of the century, those of the peasants. Without laboring the point, it is probable that student unrest in this country today is more the result of the nature and pace of change than a cause of change.

The Changing American Scene

Another profound effect over the past century of the changes we have been noting is upon our political postulates. With growing emphasis after the Civil War the principal postulate, the Zeitgeist, was faith in Progress, conceived of as a force moving humanity steadily forward and upward. So strong was faith in this escalator that interference with its workings was regarded as a sort of hubris, an insolent meddling with divine law. Indeed, the Supreme Court interpreted the constitutional protection of life, liberty, and property as incorporating the doctrine of laissez faire, or —in Justice Holmes's phrase—as enacting Mr. Herbert Spencer's *Social Statics*. Legislatures were prohibited from regulating economic enterprise in doing what came naturally.

Now, however, acceptance of the mechanistic ideal of Progress has given way to galloping nihilism and cynicism on one side and to escapist sentimentality on the other. In the resulting confusion a new postulate has easily taken over first place in political belief. The doctrine that all men are created equal has long been deeply embedded in our political holy writ. After passing through the larval and chrysalis stage as an aspiration and ritualistic affirmation, it now emerges as the crusading faith of our time, demanding destruction of infidels. Egalitarianism and its corollary, majoritarianism, are potent forces for change today. Again, the Supreme Court within the past decade and a half has given constitutional sanction to both doctrines as controlling in our domestic affairs.

The State Department verbally embraces the same

doctrines as the touchstone in relations with governments abroad. Their effects are only tangential and whimsical, for few governments in the world are based upon a broad, honest, and effective franchise. The domestic affairs of strong governments, like those of most of the communist states, we cannot affect and do not try to. Weaker regimes, such as those in Greece and Haiti, we scold for departures from the true faith. In regard to assorted regimes, black and white, the egalitarian principle is treated with light-hearted inconsistency. The black dictatorship of General Mobutu in the Congo is pampered with over a billion dollars in aid funds, while Duvalier's Haiti is starved. The white governments in southern Africa are subjected to various manifestations of displeasure (all ineffective), including embargoes and other irritations. Like a cannon loose in an eighteenth-century ship of the line during heavy weather, the principle of egalitarianism can wreak considerable havoc to the crew without harm to the enemy.

Together the electronic media and egalitarianism have intensified the change in the nature of American political leadership that began in the Jackson era. Until then—and in Europe until much later—the word "Establishment" could be meaningfully applied to those directing the nation's affairs. After Jackson, and particularly after the Civil War, the Establishment split, the controllers of economic affairs taking over the bulk of ability and power. Politicians, federal and local, fell into disrepute amounting almost to contempt. The same was true in Europe, so much so that

The Changing American Scene

George Bernard Shaw, himself a Fabian socialist, in *Back to Methuselah,* imagined a society of people living to nearly a millennium, attaining great wisdom, and assigning the duties of government to Chinese slaves. The main point, however, is the interacting effect of the demotion in status of the politician, the increase in complexity of his problems, and the development of electronic communication.

In a democracy gifts of advocacy and acting, enhanced by the new techniques of communication, are of immense importance in attaining political power and maintaining agreement, approval, and consent. They are, however, far less potent aids in the management of great affairs. Mr. Churchill's oratory inspired the British people, but it was his ability to stimulate and direct wise action that carried them through the Battle of Britain. Hitler's oratory aroused the German people, only to lead them to evil courses and their own destruction.

The needs of a politician before and after his election to office were strikingly brought home to me during a call from Mr. John F. Kennedy to discuss appointments to his cabinet in December, 1960. "I knew," he said, "almost everyone in the country who could have helped me in becoming President, but I know all too few who can help me in acting as President."

It would be quite wrong, however, to leave the impression that the chief effect of the new electronic communication is as an aid to its adept users in gaining a political following. The obverse is equally true. It is

189

also a powerful aid to the impact of any protesting group upon both political leaders and other social groups. Nor is this all. By accentuating the dramatic —and what is more dramatic than conflict?—it encourages exhibitionism, extremism, and violence. These are far more potent in gaining attention and asserting a position than reasoned argument and rational persuasion. The effect is to set aflame the atmosphere of political discourse and deprive it of reason, just as the great fire raids of the last war fed upon oxygen sucked from the air.

Finally, we are not without some experience to guide us in foreseeing the effect that competing and inflamed protests, aimed both at influencing leaders and attracting support, have upon the cohesion of a society. When I was young, British society nearly came apart over the controversy about Home Rule for Ireland and the Ulster question. Extremes of passion made parliamentary government almost impossible. Violence permeated the political scene to the point of being embraced by women in pursuit of their demand for suffrage. The loyalty of the army and of young intellectuals to "King and Country" was drawn into question. The outbreak of the First World War, perhaps, saved Britain from trouble approaching that which produced the Civil War in 1641, the Revolution of 1688, and the Chartist riots of the nineteenth century.

Not long afterward the combination of military defeat and resulting internal divisions of the most basic sort so dissolved the coherence of the Russian and German political systems that the Bolsheviks and the

Nazis, respectively, were enabled to impose their to-
talitarian systems and suppress all dissent by force and
terror.

Such are the main elements, as I see them, in the
changing American scene. What are the implications
for our future national welfare? Do they help or hinder
establishing justice, insuring domestic tranquility,
and providing for the common defense? Do they help
or hinder the conduct of relations with foreign nations
to create a favorable environment in which free societies may survive and flourish? I believe that they are
harmful for the reasons that can be briefly stated and
explained.

First, the factors of change already noted are reducing the quality of judgment and the effectiveness of
action with which our society and others deal with the
tasks confronting them. They push leaders and led toward the satisfaction of immediate desires and easiest
choices. They turn people away from self-restraint,
discipline, and pursuit of values attainable only by
persistent following of long-run policies.

Second, these same factors affect other nations very
much the same way they affect us. Thus, an ill-con-
sidered decision of one state may adversely affect another, provoking an equally ill-judged response,
impairing the long-range interests of both and the
prospects of future cooperation. Furthermore, as Lord
Salisbury observed, the world was better off when people "could read no other language than their own."
Now that they can hear and see what is going on every-

191

where, there is no end to "envy, hatred, and malice, and all uncharitableness" in interfering with other peoples' business. National and international communities are becoming more volatile, reacting hastily to find quick relief from often self-inflicted ills at the expense of impairing well-laid plans and more distant values.

For instance, during a brief period after the last war, a few gifted French leaders initiated in Western Europe inspired steps toward a unity that might transcend the confines of small national states and hold promise of a new, strong, and benign unity in world affairs. The French people tired under the immediate strains of the task. Diverted by the lure of glamour and *folie de grandeur,* they followed General de Gaulle into a policy of prideful nationalism, which the country could not economically afford or militarily support. In its course to failure the military defense of Europe was weakened, the franc devalued, and economic and political conflicts were set up within Europe and with the United States that have impaired the opportunity to create a viable European community.

Again, as one considers our increasing involvement in Vietnam following the French withdrawal in 1954, one notes a series of improvised steps to deal piecemeal with a deteriorating situation. Most of them won general approval; none appeared as a large commitment until a very large one was upon us. One senses the defect, dangerous to gamblers and politicians, of increasing one's bets and investment in a venture showing steady loss, thus increasing the difficulty of cutting one's losses and scrapping the venture. One misses a calculation of the future, a reckoning of costs within allowable investment and values obtainable, unobscured by words like "falling dominoes," "honorable solutions," and "the will to win." The result has shaken confidence in our government at home and abroad and set up or increased conflicts, dangerous in the extreme, within our society. This is a description of continued failure of judgment.

Illustrations could be multiplied. It is enough to mention the reaction of the Soviet apparatus to alarm over successful protest by the Czechs against the rigidity of their communist bureaucracy and fear that it might be contagious. The short-term solution of invasion and suppression suggests long-term setbacks in relaxing fears and hostilities that must precede settlements furthering Russian security. One can add the failures of developing societies in Latin America to identify and attack their own problems rather than protest that a rich neighbor is not doing more to help them.

Perhaps the most basic difficulties of our own society and others in this time of protest and communication arise in identifying real subjects of concern and dealing with them with discrimination, circumspection, and persistence. In his book, *The Unheavenly City*, Professor Edward C. Banfield of Harvard discusses "Counterfeit Crises and Real Problems." Confusion comes from failure to differentiate the consequences of a cold from that of cancer. Our people are overwhelmed and frustrated by a multiplicity of concerns. A danger that confronts the radar of antiballistic systems is being saturated and rendered ineffective by multitudinous incoming targets—some false, some real weapons. Survival lies in identifying the real ones. In the political and social fields, protests, demonstrations, strikes, disorder, and the Babel of media do not help separate the counterfeit and spurious from the real. Counterfeiting crises is considerably more serious than counterfeiting currency and is worthy of at least equal suppression.

When real problems are identified, the need arises to deal with them circumspectly. This requires a penetrating survey of all aspects of the problem and the effects of all solutions proposed. Solutions that create more or more serious problems than they attempt to solve are not wise or feasible, no matter how much support they have. For instance, when the legally enforced separation of black and white children for purposes of education had been identified as a problem requiring solution, it should have been recognized as different and separate from other problems, such as enforcing by law some specific racial mixture in all public schools, or the use of schools whose primary function is education, as an instrument of social reform. Careful scrutiny of remedies would reject as not feasible those that seemed likely to bring an exodus of whites from cities, impairment of the cities' tax bases, underemployment and crime within them, and decline in the quality of public education, other services, and the general urban environment.

In the foreign field the same necessity exists for discernment in selecting objectives and circumspection in choosing means and methods. Aid and trade policies and methods, for instance, seem to be products of popular whims and vagaries. Sometimes the aim asserted is to gain allies or strengthen them; at other times, to strengthen democratic regimes; at still others, to punish those of whom we disapprove by cutting trade relations. Often the object seems to be the humanitarian one of relieving need; and, again, the more earthy one of reducing surpluses by giving them away. Some urge the building of commercial bridges to communist satellites, presumably to wean them away from their ideology. In the face of this confusion, consistency in policy is almost impossible, and intelligent criticism of method very difficult. The result is most often an attitude of revulsion against liberal trade and aid policies and return to restrictive and isolationist ones.

However, "the common defense"—as the Constitution states one of our trinity of national purposes— suffers, perhaps, most severely in the interplay between the masses and the media. Here, where General Marshall used to urge that consistency and persistence in effort are as important as magnitude, policy is subject to extremes of almost hysterical pressures. Under the stimulus of actual enemy attack, there is almost no limit to what the media will support, the people will authorize, and the government will provide. When the memory of danger fades, taxation and national service are viewed as intolerable and unnecessary burdens. Distrust, springing from an unpopular war, accompanied by its full quota of military and political misjudgments, touches off an epidemic of attacks and protests, which undermine confidence in the whole military establishment. When a distinguished soldier and undistinguished president voiced suspicion of the "military-industrial complex," he proved not only that "war is much too serious a thing to be left to military men," but that politics is, also.

War—certainly nuclear war—is too serious a thing to be engaged in by anyone. The object of national policy is to prevent it. In the present state of justified mistrust among nuclear powers, endless talk alone cannot produce a reliable nuclear disarmament treaty. Verbal negotiations will have to be accompanied over many years by negotiation through acts in which a wise, expensive, and persistent military policy upon our part might convince the Russians of our mutual interest in maintaining stable second-strike capabilities on both sides, incapable of escalation into a first-strike capability without detection from outside observation.

Then, and only then, could some measure of confidence be placed in engagements. But have we the resolution and discipline to embark on and maintain such a policy over the years? Twenty years ago I argued with conviction that our society was inherently stronger than the Soviet because it was supported by the free will and consent of its citizens, whereas a communist regime rested upon compulsion backed by fear. If, however, free citizens turn against a course that their interest calls upon them to follow, within measurable time it will fail. The virus of disbelief in danger and recoil from meeting it seem to lead to distrust and impatience toward our allies and a wishful belief that Russian hostility of the Stalin-Khrushchev period has abated. Some go even further and urge a unilateral postponement in development or even an actual reduction of our military capacity to induce a Russian response in kind.

Enough has been said to indicate where present trends could take us. I cannot recall an instance of a democratic society that, once having lost the will to provide for domestic tranquility and national security, has regained it by a new birth of discipline and commitment. It has been said that the judgment of nature upon error is death. In the life of nations that judgment has been disaster. I do not predict. It is enough to regret that

> I tell you nought for your comfort,
> Yea, nought for your desire,
> Save that the sky grows darker yet,
> And the sea rises higher.

Part Five ⋘

In Memoriam

George Rublee

1868-1957

George Rublee was a great gentleman. His like we shall not see soon again. For he came from a time and an environment which has gone, and to which he added something unique from himself. He was a great gentleman in no small degree because of the Wykehamist truth that manners maketh man. What one is is more than half determined by what one does. The brave man is not only one who does not know fear but also one who has conquered the urge to run away. Whatever inner turmoils assailed George Rublee, he conducted himself with a serenity which was not just stoicism. In him it combined courtesy, gentleness—and always an elusive detachment, an aloofness even in the midst of involvement.

For me George Rublee began as a tradition—his name carved in lonely eminence on an oaken panel as

Groton Quarterly, Summer, 1957.

the first graduating class of Groton School, appearing again in the gymnasium as the captain of every team, and in the folklore of the place as the winner of prizes, the setter of standards. Years later quite unexpectedly he became a reality to me. In the same month he joined a new law firm which had just hired me. For the last thirty-five years of his life we were colleagues, partners, and friends. He was the most kind and loyal of friends.

In the fifty-odd years before I knew him as more than a tradition and an imposing figure at the Rector's table, a character of the most intriguing sort had developed. The Rublees were a Huguenot family which had long been settled in Vermont. In 1839 George's grandfather went west to Wisconsin to farm and lumber. There his son grew up, became an editor and a founder of and a power in the Republican Party of his state. There George was born in Madison about the same time as General Grant was being elected President of the United States. This event was to have significance for the child. President Grant appointed Horace Rublee Minister to Switzerland, where George's childhood was spent, and where his earliest memories and affections were centered. In Europe began the formation of his tastes and interests. After this diplomatic interlude the family lived for two years in Boston, where Mr. Rublee was the "temporary editor" of the *Daily Advertiser*. It is rumored that there was some talk of his becoming editor of the *Atlantic Monthly* at the time when the choice fell on Thomas Bailey Aldrich. At any rate the family returned to

George Rublee

Milwaukee in 1881, where the father became a part owner and the editor of the *Milwaukee Sentinel,* which he made one of the most influential and widely quoted newspapers in the whole area.

Milwaukee in those days had an atmosphere of cosmopolitan culture which few American cities have today. Its leading citizens included numbers of Germans, Swiss, and French to whom the languages, literatures, and music of Europe were natural and loved inheritances. A generation later George Kennan grew up there. His father, an officer of a land grant railroad, went yearly to northern Europe in search of immigrants to take up the railroad's land. In these travels he acquired a French and German library of distinction. Milwaukee was, Kennan has said, a community of strong, diverse, and cultivated individuals.

Here George Rublee lived until he came east to Groton and Harvard. After Harvard College, declining an invitation to teach Greek which tempted him, he returned for two years to the Europe which was always to delight him, then came back to study at the Harvard Law School. There he made three friendships which were among the closest and most enduring of his life —Edward Burling and Augustus Hand, in the class before him, and Learned Hand in the class following him. After a very brief period of teaching, on President Eliot's invitation, at the Harvard Law School he returned to Wisconsin.

But George did not share his father's zest in the life of the Middle West at the end of the century. A year of practice without clients in Milwaukee, followed by two years with Burling in Chicago, centered in the pursuit and capture of the charming Juliet Barrett, was enough. He left for the wider and more glamorous life of New York to practice with the leading authority on corporations, Victor Morawetz.

Now began, as in a symphony, the movement first indistinct and faltering, then repeated with growing clarity and insistence, which was to dominate George Rublee's life, a movement with alternating themes, one of contented languor touched with melancholy, the other a passionate, almost demoniacal seizure which carried him to heights of brilliant and tireless effort, ending in the tragedy of frustration and failure, followed again by the melancholy languor.

The work in New York was hardly begun when George, by fortunate investment, made, for those days, a comfortable fortune. He promptly retired from practice and took his pretty wife to Europe, where, universally admired, the couple moved in social, artistic, and sporting circles. George became the favorite tennis partner of the late King of Sweden. His wife danced and charmed. Several years passed and some of the fortune. The champagne of life began to go flat. The Rublees returned to New York to practice law again, this time with the late Joseph P. Cotton and Senator John C. Spooner of Wisconsin.

Then came the first of the seizures. In 1910 the Progressives and Young Turks were in full revolt against President Taft and, most especially and particularly, against his Secretary of the Interior, Richard A. Ballinger. The Robin Hood of this adventure was

George Rublee

Gifford Pinchot; the St. George was Louis D. Brandeis, retained by *Collier's Weekly* to conduct the case against Secretary Ballinger before the Senate Committee investigating charges against him. Rublee became St. George's squire.

The story is too long to tell in all its details. The dilettante of the previous year was inexhaustible, infinitely resourceful, passionately committed. The dragon was slain. The Taft administration was mortally hurt. The Bull Moose sounded his call and George marched to Armageddon with T. R. through the Chicago convention, the creation of the Square Deal, persuading his leader on the way first to transfer his advocacy of the recall of judges to the recall of judicial decisions, and then to soft-pedal the whole matter—all to the martial strains of "Onward Christian Soldiers." The crescendo mounted, then crashed to disaster, complete, total, absolute. There was a breathless moment of silence. Then began again the theme of quiet melancholy.

This time it was shorter. Brandeis sent for him again. Together they worked out for the new professor President the first of his prophylactic antitrust measures, the Federal Trade Commission Act. Again he was the tireless lobbyist for rectitude, the battler against odds, the persuader, the inexhaustible one. The Act was passed. Rublee was named the first Chairman of the Federal Trade Commission. Senator Gallinger of New Hampshire, where he had his residence, stated that Rublee was personally obnoxious to him. The Administration threw in its reserves and was defeated by senatorial courtesy. Again crescendo, again the silence.

Three years went by and the First World War burst upon an astonished America. Rublee's sympathies were quick and strong. He was soon deeply committed. His friend Raymond B. Stevens of New Hampshire, who had been a member of Congress and an ally in the Federal Trade Commission battle, had become Vice Chairman of the United States Shipping Board. At Stevens's invitation Rublee joined in that great innovation in international organization, the Allied Maritime Transport Council, where, through a skilled staff of civil servants, which included that amazing person Jean Monnet, allied shipping tonnage was pooled and allocated for war use. At Rublee's suggestion, Dwight W. Morrow joined the American mission. Purely as war work the task was absorbing. Gradually a vision as mystical and inspired as that of the Holy Grail began to come to this brilliant and devoted group. It seemed to them that here in this body of disciplined men, a technical staff, might lie the secret of subordinating national interests in the creation of a new world order. Reason and knowledge could be, they thought, so powerful as to overwhelm prejudice and narrow interest.

As the war ended conviction grew, and Rublee, with the others, threw himself into the fight for the League of Nations with a passion transcending anything he had experienced before. Again the end was the same. Again all was turned to dust, ashes, and frustration.

More than a decade passed before the spirit pos-

George Rublee

sessed him again. During this time he turned more and more to his beloved classics (in the original, with a handy trot), to his friends, to his walks at Cornish, New Hampshire. In the wider world he took on a few interesting tasks, but nothing which stirred him. He went with his partners to an arbitration at The Hague; with Mr. Morrow to Mexico, where his ingenuity and persistence were instrumental in reconciling the Mexican government and the Church; to Colombia, where he worked out an oil code for that government.

In 1938 President Roosevelt persuaded Rublee to become director of the Intergovernmental Committee on Refugees, which was attempting by negotiation with Nazi Germany to save by emigration the German Jews. Once again the magnitude of the cause fired George Rublee to overcome towering obstacles. One difficulty after another was met, as conference followed conference up the Nazi hierarchical scale. At last the impossible seemed accomplished. At Hitler's direction Goering was made the Fuehrer's deputy with power to act. George threw himself into the final effort. He believed that he had won Goering over. The Red Sea seemed to have parted to open the way to a new deliverance. Then came the war, and the deaths of six million people in the concentration camps and gas chambers of Germany and the ghettos of Poland.

This was the last passion; the fire, even in the inner recesses of his nature, had gone out. Here in this summary we have the mystery of a man's life. That George Rublee had gifts far beyond those given to most able men cannot be doubted. But why was he fully extended

207

so intermittently? Why did his potentiality so often seem to elude him? Who can say? Perhaps the favor of fortune and the admiration of men—and women, too —was a handicap when it seemed such an advantage. Perhaps the discipline of a harder environment, where he would not have been so acclaimed but would have been pushed and buffeted by urgent necessities would have made dominant those qualities which, on occasion, could burst into blazing possession of him.

I have seen it happen in a moment. For weeks I had worked preparing him for an argument at The Hague. At times it was hard to get his attention; he seemed often diffident, unsure, listless. The day came. As he mounted the pulpit-like advocate's stand in the Peace Palace, he was a man I had never seen. Confident, even arrogant in his assertive power, he dominated the room. His usually quiet voice rang with authority. He pushed his notes aside and told that tribunal exactly what it was called upon to do.

Would he have been as beloved if he had attained his full potentiality? I think undoubtedly not. For, although he always seemed to slip from one's grasp into his own pavilion, few men have ever so absorbed the interest and devotion of their friends. He was a great and gallant gentleman.

Edward B. Burling

1870-1966

It is an intimidating experience for me to speak about Ned Burling, not only because he was a dear friend, but because I can always see that humorous, warm, twinkle in his eye fastened on me, that cynical smile which has been caught so well in the painting which is in our 7th floor reception room and in Mrs. Burling's house—you all know it—and once that look is fixed on you, you cannot be stuffy, you cannot be sentimental, and moreover, you cannot be untrue.

I would not dare to say anything about Ned Burling that I had not said to his face, and so I start off with an insult I used to give him all the time, saying that he was a complete fraud and that he put on a front of being tough, and worldly, and cynical, and brutal, as

Remarks delivered at the Memorial Services at the Washington Cathedral, Washington, D.C. October 4, 1966.

though that was the man; it wasn't at all. This was a complete false front. He had those qualities; he could be tough; he was worldly on occasion; he knew the world, but no one in my experience has ever been so generous, so warm, so compassionate, so interested in people about him, their lives, their careers, their worries, and everything that went on, as the man that all of you, all of the older ones of you, at any rate, have called Uncle Ned.

He picked the older ones out himself. As John O'Brian and Bill Jones said this morning, he was the one who staffed the early office. When I came along three years after the office had started and had been in there a little while, I had the first job of bringing to his attention young men, and the young men I brought to his attention—I know they seem to you old, but then they were very young indeed—all of them will remember their first interviews with Ned Burling, his prodding of them to see whether behind that certificate of membership on the Law Review there was humanity, whether they had other interests, whether they were concerned about anything except the books in the library.

Yes, his great interest, outside of his family, of course, was the firm. The outstanding quality of his interest was the vast generosity, which in a very short time took the first of us whom he brought in into partnership, and then, not long after that, and not long after Judge Covington's death, turned over the firm to us.

He watched it carefully, he loved it, it was his great

absorbing interest. He was interested in everybody in it. Not particularly the brightest people. He wasn't so much concerned with standing in the law school. He was, perhaps, more interested in the two qualities that he always looked for: Were they interested in their clients, were they doing a lawyer's job for a client, or were they trying to write Law Review articles. He was interested in the former and not the latter.

Then, did they have other interests outside of law? John O'Brian spoke about that this morning. Ned was at heart a romantic. This I think explains his great friendship with Tom Corcoran—who is the greatest romantic in Washington today. Tom brought to Ned the world as a story, sometimes a world which perhaps did not exist, sometimes a world which did, but always as a story he found absorbing.

He used to prod me about my adventures in the world. He always sent me off to the adventures in which I engaged, and when I would come back, or while I was still engaged in them, he would pump me dry and say, "What went on?" "Who said what to whom, who fired the first shot," et cetera. He was deeply, deeply interested in the people around him and in the world around him. And above all, at the very basis of his relationships to people and his relationships with the firm, was generosity and deep abiding concern for all people.

He regarded the law not as something interesting in itself, but as a tool. To him it was only a good tool if it was a sharp and accurate tool, and he wanted that; but he wanted, as I said earlier, more than that, that the

In Memoriam

firm be a practical organization, engaged in achieving practical ends, for real people, who were in real trouble, and when he saw that the firm was good at that, and was getting a greater and greater reputation in the country. it gave him great happiness. This, I am sure, he leaves to you, and this I am sure you will carry on as he would have wished it to be carried on.

Mr. Justice Brandeis

1856-1941

In this moment of farewell to the Justice, I should like to speak very briefly of what he has meant in the lives of a score of men who have had the great joy and the great fortune of serving him so intimately as his secretaries. We are the fortunate ones, but what he has meant to us is not very different from what he has meant to hundreds of young men and women who have grown up under his influence. We are scattered over the country, some are on the bench, some are teaching, some are in the practice of law, some are in the service of the government. But today to all of us there comes a surge of memories. It is almost impossible from among the strands of memory to select those which are most significant, but there are two strands, I

Remarks delivered at the funeral services, October 7, 1941, Washington, D.C. Published in *Harvard Law Review,* vol. 55, No. 2, December, 1941.

believe, which have been woven deeply into our lives.

I need not say how great an influence upon us it was to begin our work under the guiding hand of the Justice and to know the brilliance of his mind, but our relationship was far more than that between young men and one of the greatest and most revered figures of our time. What gave it life, what gave it endurance was the depth of affection which the warmth of his interest and solicitude for us inspired. Throughout these years we have brought him all our problems and all our troubles, and he had time for all of us. In talk with him the problems answered themselves. A question, a comment, and the difficulties began to disappear; the dross and shoddy began to appear for what it was, and we wondered why the matter had ever seemed difficult.

I have talked, over the past twenty years, with the Justice about these men. I have heard him speak of some achievement of one of us with all the pride and of some sorrow or disappointment of another with all the tenderness of a father speaking of his sons. He entered so deeply into our lives because he took us so deeply into his.

The other strand in these memories is all the more vivid because of the times in which we have lived. We are the generation which has lived during and between two wars. We have lived in the desert years of the human spirit. We have lived in the barren years of disillusionment—years when the cry was "What is truth?" —years when men with a little new-found knowledge believed that they had pried into the mainsprings of the human mind and spirit, and could make mankind work for any end by playing upon its fears and appetites.

These were years during which we were with the Justice and saw in action his burning faith that the verities to which men had clung through the ages were verities; that evil never could be good; that falsehood was not truth, not even if all the ingenuity of science reiterated it in waves that encircled the earth.

We have heard him say almost in the words of St. Paul, "Whatsoever things are true, whatsoever things are honest, whatsoever things are just, whatsoever things are pure, whatsoever things are of good report —think on these things."

But to him truth was less than truth unless it were expounded so that people could understand and believe. During these years of retreat from reason, his faith in the human mind and in the will and capacity of people to understand and grasp the truth never wavered or tired. In a time of moral and intellectual anarchy and frustration he handed on the great tradition of faith in the mind and spirit of man which is the faith of the prophets and poets, of Socrates, of Lincoln.

And so today, whatever dark days may lie ahead, the memory of the Justice will be a voice always saying to us, "Lift up your hearts!"

Norman Hapgood

1868-1937

Thursday, March 28, was the centennial anniversary of the birth of Norman Hapgood. All too few of us are left who knew and were warmed by the friendship of that gay, vibrant and perennially young spirit. His views of the world about him, simpler, clearer and healthier than ours today, were those of the "Progressive Era" which produced him.

I first knew Norman Hapgood fifty years ago, when the peak of his journalistic career was over. He was, as the Wilson years faded to an end, entering the Great Sanhedrin of his profession, the glorious company of columnists, for which he was congenitally unfitted by reason of doubting something of his own infallibility, in Franklin's phrase, and of an aversion to pomposity.

Though the active days were past, he re-created

The New York Times, March 31, 1968.

them in his delightful talk, introducing me to the
adult life of a time I had spent in the nursery and in
school. These years he had lived in a New York where
flourished Society with a capital S, understandable
art, political bosses, scandals and reform, where crime
waves had just been discovered but teachers' and gar-
bage collectors' strikes had not.

What I heard most were tales of his long association
with my boss when I first came to Washington, Justice
Louis D. Brandeis. For years they were embattled as
what some would have described as crusaders against
corruption and conspiracy against the public interest,
and others as "muckrakers." Hapgood enlisted in the
crusade against Charles S. Mellen and the New Haven
Railroad's monopoly of rail, ship and trolley transportation in New England, beginning the long vendetta
between Brandeis and what we would now call "the
Establishment."

In the next crusade—the Ballinger investigation—
the two friends found combined in rare degree the two
essential elements of muckraking—fraud and drama. It
also taught an important lesson of politics: that saints
are canonized for slaying serpents and dragons, but
not kings. The Ballinger investigation grew out of a
row between Richard Ballinger, President Taft's Secretary of the Interior, and Gifford Pinchot, chief
forester of the Department of Agriculture, over some
public lands in Alaska that President Roosevelt had
withdrawn from sale and that Ballinger proposed to
restore to sale. Hapgood obtained and published a report to Secretary Ballinger by a junior official, Louis
R. Glavis, which the author had given to the President.

Brandeis, representing Glavis, suspected the unbelievable. With Hapgood's help, he proved that a President of the United States and his Attorney General had had prepared, antedated, and inserted into the record of a presidential decision exonerating Ballinger a document that had not existed at the time of the decision, yet had been put forward as its cause. After proof, the fact was admitted by the participants.

The blast effect of this amazing performance was wide, and destructive of President Taft's chances of re-election in 1912. It also contributed in 1916 to the opinion by Mr. Taft and others that Mr. Brandeis was "not a fit person to be a member of the Supreme Court."

Norman Hapgood and Louis Brandeis supported a Progressive, Robert La Follette, for the Republican nomination in 1912, and when that failed they switched to Wilson in the election. In 1916 Hapgood was endlessly resourceful in meeting the calumnies of the long fight against the Brandeis nomination to the Supreme Court.

Norman Hapgood was not made for the complexities of the confused times between the wars—if, indeed, any one was. The gay spirit of a journalistic Robin Hood was inadequate to take successfully from the oppressive rich for the oppressed poor, or to see very clearly which was which. But Norman Hapgood's companionship remained a joy, his spirit combative and happy.

He was spared a long decline and went down with all lights burning and the band playing, the happy survivor of a happier age.

Felix Frankfurter

1882-1965

It has been said of Leslie Stephen, by Mait-
land, I think, that those who did not know him would
never understand the source and magnitude of his influence. For that reason he would be an enigma to
future generations. Reading his written words would
give a quite inadequate, often erroneous, impression
of the man, and no sense at all of the effect on the
hearer of the spoken word. This is preeminently true
of Felix Frankfurter. One could read everything that
he has written—a formidable task from several points
of view—and still have little more than an inkling, if
that, of why this man has evoked in so many such passionate devotion and exercised for half a century so
profound an influence. I can think of no one in our
time remotely comparable to him, though it would not
surprise me if in another time Dr. Franklin might
have had something of the same personal influence.

Harvard Law Review, vol. 76, No. 1, November, 1962.

In Memoriam

In the same way, the words, especially the written words, of another cannot convey the reality of Felix Frankfurter. There is no substitute for the apprehension of the senses. One needs to see, to hear—particularly to hear his laugh, his general noisiness—to realize what an obstreperous person this man is, to have one's arm numbed by his vise-like grip just above one's elbow, to feel the intensity of his nervous energy. Above all one needs years of experience to know the depth of his concern about people. He lives in personal relationships as a fish lives in water. This is no secluded scholar immured in library or laboratory, absorbed in intellectual problems, but a man immersed in people. At a moment's notice he will concentrate his mind and heart on their interests, their joys, or their troubles.

It has been said that Felix Frankfurter has a genius for friendship. This is not only true, but true by reason of the basic quality from which genius springs. He has an infinite capacity for taking pains about his friendships. He elevates friendship from a vague consciousness of being sympathetic with another person to an art which he practices assiduously. He thinks a great deal about his friends, talks about them with other friends, worries about them if they are unhappy or unfortunate, praises them, sometimes chides them. When he comes across something which would interest one of them, off goes a note or a clipping. He spends hours talking with them on the telephone; he must be a mainstay of the telephone company.

The other passion of his life, an avidity for good talk, only swells his absorption in people, so that a friendship which is old and tried, where talk flows easily and common interests are many and vigorous, can become for both parties utter joy. For twenty years we walked downtown together every fair day. My wife would speculate in amazement on what we could find to talk about for an hour every morning and during a telephone call or visit in the evening. Yet the talk never stopped and never ceased to absorb us. For one reason everything he begins to say brings in something else, parenthesis forms within parenthesis; the texture of the narrative becomes incomparably rich, varied, gay, fascinating in content. I remember what started to be a simple statement, to the effect that someone we knew did something, begun one morning as we started out and completed fourteen blocks later, with encyclopedic and delightful embroidery detailing the history of all the relatives and other connections of everyone involved. As time went on, our inability to stop our talk at the Pennsylvania Avenue entrance to the old State Department led to amused comment, which drove us to an agreement that we would stop, even in the middle of a sentence, as we passed a certain crack in the sidewalk. But it was no use. He claimed that to stop walking, but not talking, when we came to the crack, was only proper avoidance, and not illegal evasion, of the rule.

I have heard Felix Frankfurter vigorous in argument; and know that his replies are often sharp, though never with me. Norman Hapgood used to say that F. F. enjoyed nothing so much as to win in argument and by unfair means, if possible. But this, I think, came from Norman's frustration, himself a witty and adroit dialectician, at always being outpointed.

In Memoriam

Judge Hand was right in the view attributed to him, when F. F. said to me one day, "What do you bet that B says of me when I'm not present, 'Sure you can differ with him, but the little cuss is honest.'"

F. F. has a way with children. He treats them formally and seriously (again reminiscent of Dr. Franklin); they respond with unembarrassed directness. When this directness turns the tables on him, he is delighted. Years ago he came to our house to call on a family staying with us. The parents were out, but the "dulcet and harmonious breath" of a recorder, expertly played, floated down from the second floor. F. F. followed it to a bedroom where the young son of our guests was nursing a cold. As the stranger appeared, the lad stopped his playing and looked up. "Peter," said F. F., "I'm a friend of your parents and a Justice of the Supreme Court; but I would rather be able to make music as you do than be a judge."

"So would I," said Peter.

F. F. was delighted. "Good, wasn't it?" he would shout as he told the story again and again.

To our own children over three decades, and now to grandchildren, he has been an ever beloved, understanding, and gay friend. During the war a stream of letters, clippings, and court opinions went to the Pacific to nourish our sons' days and months on a destroyer; and to the girls, too, with trials of their own, he was an ever present help.

Over the years a phrase keeps coming to my mind which seems to give the essence of my friend. It is the title of a book which I read long ago, *The Loving Spirit.*